"With *Getting Innovation Right*, Seth has delivered a guide for leaders everywhere to help accelerate their team's innovation through real-world examples and pragmatic insight."

—Kevin Parker; president, CEO, and chairman of the board, Deltek, Inc.

"As a client of Seth's I am happy he has written a book that spells out the successes he has had with a number of organizations. There are great lessons here. He took on tough challenges and turned them into success stories. *Getting Innovation Right* will resonate far beyond the industries his book covers. We can all learn from others' success when it comes to innovation."

—Ralph Nappi, president, The Association for Suppliers of Printing, Publishing and Converting Technologies

"Seth is a boundless strategic thinker and motivator. *Getting Innovation Right* can propel your organization's next move upward. Finding that elusive formula is the key to achieving sustainable, profitable revenue growth, and Seth gets the job done in an entertaining way."

—Mike Panaggio, chairman, DME Holdings, LLC

"Seth does it again with his latest book, *Getting Innovation Right*, by providing a simple approach to attacking innovation. It is having the courage to innovate that will differentiate us from all the rest and is what we all strive for. After reading this book, you will not only have an approach to utilize, but the tools to help you make things happen quickly and succeed."

—Michaela Oliver, senior vice president of human resources, Rosetta Stone, Inc.

"*Getting Innovation Right* emphasizes a maturity that all business executives should develop. I highly recommend this book, as it captures both basic business fundamentals and a dynamic approach for executives to rethink processes and strategy on an ongoing basis."

—Anthony J. Cancelosi, K.M., president and CEO, Columbia Lighthouse for the Blind

"In this massively disruptive and mostly distracting business environment, you have but one choice: innovate, or evaporate. But you must get it right, which isn't easy. Enter Seth Kahan's *Getting Innovation Right*."

—Matthew E. May, author, *The Laws of Subtraction* and *The Shibumi Strategy*

J JOSSEY-BASS™
A Wiley Brand

GETTING INNOVATION RIGHT

HOW LEADERS LEVERAGE INFLECTION POINTS TO DRIVE SUCCESS

Seth Kahan

WILEY

Cover concept by Faceout Studio

Published by Jossey-Bass
A Wiley Imprint
One Montgomery Street, Suite 1200, San Francisco, CA 94104-4594 — www.josseybass.com

Jossey-Bass books and products are available through most bookstores. To contact Jossey-Bass directly call our Customer Care Department within the U.S. at 800-956-7739, outside the U.S. at 317-572-3986, or fax 317-572-4002.

Wiley publishes in a variety of print and electronic formats and by print-on-demand. Some material included with standard print versions of this book may not be included in e-books or in print-on-demand. If this book refers to media such as a CD or DVD that is not included in the version you purchased, you may download this material at http://booksupport.wiley.com. For more information about Wiley products, visit www.wiley.com.

Library of Congress Cataloging-in-Publication Data
Kahan, Seth.
  Getting innovation right : how leaders leverage inflection points to drive success / Seth Kahan. -- First edition.
       pages cm
  Includes bibliographical references and index.
  ISBN 978-1-118-37833-5 (cloth); ISBN 978-1-118-46144-0 (ebk); ISBN 978-1-118-46143-3 (ebk.); ISBN 978-1-118-46142-6 (ebk.)
  1. Strategic planning. 2. Technological innovations--Management. 3. Diffusion of innovations. 4. New products. 5. Leadership. I. Title.
  HD30.28.K335 2013
  658.4'063 — dc23
                                                                                            2012048517

Printed in the United States of America
FIRST EDITION

HB Printing   10 9 8 7 6 5 4 3 2 1

For visionary leaders of all kinds: may these tools and techniques help you innovate successfully for the benefit of all life.

Contents

List of Figures and Tables

Introduction

Innovation is about success. It is not innovation if you come up with something new and it cripples or kills you. If you pour in your effort and are only marginally better off than when you started, you have not achieved innovation.

Innovation is the successful introduction of a market offering that profits everybody involved, both you and your customers. Innovation happens when a new product or service creates a return in the market that far exceeds the time and money it takes to develop and execute. When a new offering is accepted and embraced, generating the resources that make it possible to support and grow its place in the market—that is innovation. That's a positive inflection point. That is what you must aim for.

I once worked on an initiative that was destined for greatness. My team at the World Bank was building a cutting edge internal network and our timing could not have been better. We called it *knowledge management*; it was a new term that highlighted the value of knowledge. It was our intention to bring knowledge management to life through the private internal communications network we were developing.

Our staff members around the world were clamoring for greater connectivity. We brought in the best of the best to design our intranet, the face of our internal network. We had highly paid, well-recognized, and experienced experts applying their best efforts.

We recruited content providers from within our ranks through a careful winnowing process that ensured we had relevant topics with excellent intellectual property. We enrolled technically savvy professionals to help us build a network that everyone would be able to put to good use. We had high hopes of forever changing the way our organization worked, uniting our people, and providing them with the knowledge they needed exactly when they needed it through the miracle of technology.

And yet it flopped. It failed in a big way. We built it and they did not come. We had created a comprehensive taxonomy — it looked like the index of the *Encyclopedia Britannica*. We had mapped every major topic area in the organization and all the corresponding nooks and crannies. The problem was they were mostly empty because the taxonomy was so large and initial participation was small. As a result when people went looking for content they came up empty-handed most of the time. This turned them off and they stopped using the system.

Even though we had a very cool system — the geeks loved it — even though we had made major progress in creating the taxonomy that would eventually catalog the Bank's internal knowledge, it was not an innovation. It did not succeed with our customers. It did not generate the value we needed to justify support and growth.

We had done a poor job of engaging our customers, the people we built the system for. There were about 12,000 people inside our organization who we hoped would be active and engaged in the new system. We had less than a hundred who understood what we were doing and only a fraction of them participating heavily. Our engagement tactics had been weak at best. As a result we were unsuccessful at creating something new that people used. Instead we had a well-developed, cutting-edge service that sat mostly dormant.

Meanwhile just down the hall in the same building where we were working, another, less dramatic effort was going on. A single man, Steve Denning, with no budget was cobbling together bits and pieces of other people's efforts with some unique ideas of his own to create a different way of doing business for the World Bank.

Steve was putting together what would become the Bank's first successful knowledge management initiative. He was playing with a fundamental innovation in the way our $20 billion a year organization carried out its core activities by leveraging knowledge as our primary asset rather than relying on what was in the vault. This was a change from a traditional bank model that relied on the forecasting of investment returns to guide the process of loaning money. Instead of focusing on the World Bank as loan processor, Steve was looking at the Bank as a global poverty alleviator. It was a radical, far-reaching idea. It was also in line with the organization's true mission in a way that traditional banking was not.

Steve's innovation was not high tech. It was social. Because it was built around the experience and expertise of people, it was realized in communities of professionals we called *Thematic Groups*. When it became clear to me that the new intranet was going nowhere, I left that effort and ended up down the hall on Steve's team.

It was 1997 when we realized that Thematic Groups were key to our success. This is where the action was: informal groups of people working together, sharing what they know, and applying it to the toughest problems they were facing. It was a major innovation for the World Bank—these groups were practically nonexistent at the time. In fact, I would say the organization was toxic to them, putting them out of business wherever and whenever they began to form.

When we initially went looking for them we had a hard time finding them because they were off the grid. We discovered them in the cafeteria or the bar across the street, but they were extremely rare in conference rooms. We had to invent new ways of working, create new jobs that didn't exist before (like community builder and knowledge analyst), confront entrenched systems and business processes that were antithetical to our goals, drive uptake (the absorption of new ways of working), help people get and demonstrate results, and convince hostile senior managers that the new ways of working were better than the existing state of affairs. It wasn't easy work.

But we did it and it paid off quickly. By the summer of 1998 there were over one hundred Thematic Groups up and running across the planet. Their work was producing dramatic results in line with the Bank's mission of poverty alleviation. We were experiencing major success—the returns on our hard work was overwhelming. We had created a positive inflection point.

We collected the stories and used them to convey the Thematic Groups' successes. It became clear that these communities were exceptionally effective at pushing the Bank's mission forward. Collectively they were a global force advancing our cause. From environmental sustainability to nutrition and health care, from infrastructure development to disaster response, these Thematic Groups were getting results on the ground.

By outside accounts the effort was a success also. Stories upon stories were being told about victories this new way of working was making possible. For example, we had leaders in Central and South America, Africa, and Asia working together to share and implement successful innovations in urban renewal, serving the urban poor. This was an area that had been extremely challenged in the past. Case studies about successes like this were being spread far and wide by other organizations. We received international recognition and praise. A panel of outside experts studied our efforts in 1999 and concluded that the Thematic Groups were "the heart and soul"[1] of our successful knowledge management program. The success we experienced resulted in $60 million of annual allocation.

More important, our success persisted after we left.

A study was conducted twelve years later. This was eight years after the team I was on disbanded. It also happened after institutional budgets had swung back and forth more than once, after the glow of our novelty had worn off, after two presidents of our organization had come and gone, and after knowledge management had swung out of favor, back in, and out again. After all this turmoil—the dramatic changing of the guards at the top of the organization, and the regular reallocation of funding to other activity—an assessment was done to learn what had happened to these groups. The study showed that ninety-six Thematic Groups remained and said "much good work is being done."[2]

This was my first big lesson in what it takes to get innovation right. It is not enough to bring in experts, strike at the ripe time, encourage creativity and freewheeling experiments, hold a tolerance for mistakes and failures, play, and cultivate intuition and curiosity. To succeed you must master the activities required to create the kind of products and services that get traction and grow, bringing you significant and measurable success in your market.

Some will tell you innovation is about good ideas. In my experience there are plenty of great ideas floating around, untested, untried, and unimplemented. A great idea is simply not enough to get you through the obstacles that new notions, products, and services inevitably raise or confront. The real trick is building something people are compelled to use or acquire, getting it into their hands in a form they can put to use, all the while moving ever more firmly into the black. I define innovation as *the creation and successful delivery of new products and services.*

I work with leaders all the time who have ideas they know will improve their customers' experience. But it seems they fall short when it comes to important details. They don't invest in the internal capacity required to successfully develop new products and services. They don't do market research to ensure circumstances are conducive to their new offering. They don't take advantage of disruption and use it to best effect. They don't think through the value from the customers' point of view. They don't drive the required uptake to increase and accelerate market acceptance. These are all things I will show you how to do in the pages ahead.

The truth is that, as a result of misguided effort, intentions often come to naught, or worse, waste precious resources. That's why I wrote this book, to highlight the activities you must engage in to drive success in the marketplace for your innovations.

Seven Key Activities for Getting Innovation Right

In my experience since 1998 working hand-in-hand with over a hundred leaders and their organizations, I have distilled seven key activities that lead to successful innovation. Leaders who carry them out put themselves ahead of their peers and the competition. The vast majority of executives do not practice any one of these with discipline or emotional intensity. Yet it is these activities that make the difference between those who are haphazardly shooting in the dark with good ideas and those who consistently and systematically uncover potential, capitalize on opportunity, and generate traction that drives success in the marketplace. By simply taking just one and putting it into practice you are putting the odds on your side. When you combine them, bringing them all to bear on your efforts, the result is an advantage that stacks many variables in your favor.

The Seven Key Activities to Getting Innovation Right are

1. **Pursue Inflection Points**. A positive inflection point is a decisive, favorable shift in your relationship to the market. Expert innovators are able to sense the potential of a positive inflection point and drive activity to stimulate or take advantage of these dramatic events. When harnessed they are like waves that propel you forward, growing your base, increasing the offerings your customers buy, generating loyalty, and moving you up-market.
2. **Build Innovation Capacity**. The systematic development of new products and services generates inherent stress. Strong innovation leaders recognize this and intentionally build the capacity to contain and channel these pressures. They do this by building the necessary foundation of internal leadership, talent, and idea management.
3. **Collect Intelligence**. The best innovation rises from a sea of products, services, customers, competitors, market conditions, and internal capabilities. To play to advantage you must consistently collect and apply pertinent information, thus systematically enhancing the quality of your strategic decisions.

4. **Shift Perspective**. In order to see new opportunity you must be able to get out of your own box. There are proven techniques and tactics capable innovators use to question their own assumptions. This allows them to see the world through alternative and helpful points of view. Learning to apply these techniques and tactics to your business will help you find new areas for innovation.

5. **Exploit Disruption**. Disruption is part of business life today. Successful leaders know how to identify the opportunity embedded in adverse conditions and exploit it. They systematically and consistently turn turmoil to their advantage.

6. **Generate Value**. Value is what causes people to separate from their hard-earned cash. It is what drives investors to invest, shoppers to shop, and people to fly around the world just to trade with each other. Skillful innovators understand what drives value, what it looks like to customers and all their stakeholders, and how to generate it by delivering something more, better, or new.

7. **Drive Innovation Uptake**. Every stage of the innovation process holds opportunity to introduce new ideas into the market and engage the community of people who will be most interested in your offerings. Uptake, or market acceptance, occurs through the well-tended generation of mutual value. Innovation leaders intentionally drive uptake, seeking to control adoption for maximum effect.

In the chapters ahead I will explore each of these seven activities one by one. Along the way I will provide tools and techniques you can put to use immediately. Follow the templates, guidelines, and step-by-step instructions and you will be best prepared to successfully innovate; that is, drive success in your market. That is where the gold is, not in my words but in your application.

Since 1997 I have worked with leaders in over sixty organizations, including Shell, World Bank, NASA, Prudential Retirement, Arent Fox, American Geophysical Union, American College of Cardiology, National Apartment Association, Johns Hopkins University Applied

Physics Laboratory, Peace Corps, and the HR Certification Institute. The techniques I present are based on real-life experience with CEOs, executive directors, and senior managers of these world-class organizations and others developing new products and services and delivering successfully to market.

My work is about getting results for my clients. I have written this book for them so they can learn from each other and for you so you can take what is here and put it to good use. It is designed to provide you with the explanations and devices you need to make the best possible impact.

I know that humanity occasionally rises to potential and achieves miracles worthy of the human spirit. We can innovate and change things for the better. Our collective efforts in that regard give me hope. For that reason I wrote what I think is a practical book, not one filled with suppositions and hypotheses. Instead I want it to be full of methods you can put to work and stories that recount direct experience so you can figure out how best to apply the material to your situation. Take what you can. Adapt it to your situation. Find satisfaction in the process and results.

Imagine what your tomorrow will be like when your ideas come to life as sustained successes. Let me help you make that a reality.

Seth Kahan
Washington, DC

GETTING INNOVATION RIGHT

Pursue and Leverage Inflection Points

A n inflection point is a dramatic and decisive shift in your relationship with the market for better or worse. It can be positive, increasing your success, or negative, as you fall out of favor. Masterful leaders anticipate inflection points and use them to their advantage, like using a wave's energy to carry them to a new and better position or preparing for a setback in conditions to minimize damage to their position. Because an inflection point springs from your relationship to the market, the change it brings comes about one of three ways: (1) you move in relation to the market, (2) the market moves in relation to you, or (3) you move in relation to each other.

Most inflection points fall in the third category, simply because conditions are constantly changing—both yours and the market's. In fact, you are a subset of the market, so change on either side results in change on both sides. But it is helpful to think in terms of the first two to get a handle on how to use market shifts to your advantage. This is done either by anticipating a major change in conditions (the market moves) or by planning a decisive pivot that puts you in a better position to succeed (you move).

An example of the market moving in relation to an organization, generating a negative inflection point, is the recent demise of the Visiting Nurse Foundation (VNF), a nonprofit that served stroke victims in Pittsburgh. VNF, founded in 1989, had as its primary revenue source the administration of flu shots. In 2007 state legislators passed a law permitting pharmacists to give flu injections and the organization's main source of funding dwindled severely.[1] The legislative process was transparent and the coming inflection point would have been visible to anyone who was looking—apparently they were not looking. As a result VNF failed to build other revenue sources and the change led to their demise.

An example of an organization designed from the beginning to create a positive inflection point is Gazelle.com. As of this writing they are the US leader in re-commerce,[2] a business founded on buying old or expired electronics so consumers can buy the latest and greatest. Re-commerce as a successful innovation was officially recognized in 2005,[3] and Gazelle.com was founded in 2006 to take advantage of it. They have achieved dramatic and consistent success with 2011 year-over-year growth of 65%.[4]

Discovering inflection points in their early stages is a powerful ally to successful innovation. But this is often easier said than done. It takes leaders who understand the power of inflection points, who invest their time and direct their staff to seek out the signals that portend significant changes, and who direct their organizations to respond strategically.

One client of mine discovered how difficult it can be to cut through the mind-set that prevents sensing an emerging inflection point. Yet as you will see, turning a potential negative into a positive inflection point can be done.

I had been hired to work with a large oil and gas operation in the Americas to determine the value of new technology that had been mandated by headquarters. This was the 2000s and every major exploration and production company was putting technology *down hole*, deep in the ground, to better monitor and model what could be extracted.

The technology was a major innovation, a breakthrough in how oil and gas was identified and existing oil wells and gas fields were optimized to produce more. Further, this breakthrough was generating a global inflection point. As underground digital technology became available around the world, oil and gas operations that adopted it gained a financial edge — my client's competitors among them.

Yet some of the folks in the Americas remained unconvinced of its utility, and as the top-producing division of the company's global operations, their resistance was significant. If they denied the inflection point, not only would they lose the value of the innovation at the cash register, they could also stall the enterprise's progress around the world and put themselves at a major disadvantage in the industry.

On the other hand, if they saw the inflection point and jumped on it, the new technology had the power to propel significant increases in the amount of oil and gas they retrieved from existing wells and fields, with great impact for the financial success of the entire enterprise, propelling them forward as global leader.

The inflection point had been identified at headquarters, but the folks in the Americas did not see it yet. To them, it seemed like just another mandate from above.

Everything came to a head in a meeting I called, bringing the two groups together. We assembled in New Orleans. Major players were present. The first two hours were civil even though it was clear that there was a rift. Slowly the two sides engaged and argued until finally we reached a point where the tension was palpable.

I thought the guy from the Gulf of Mexico was going to jump out of his chair and throttle the analyst from headquarters. "You expect me to believe those numbers? I don't trust those numbers and I don't trust you because you gave me those numbers. There is no way in hell that you can tell me you know what this technology will do. There are just too many variables at play. Is that what you believe? I mean do *you* believe these numbers?"

The room was dead quiet. Everyone waited to see what the analyst from headquarters would say.

It had been two years since headquarters had mandated the new technology that could produce exceptional results. But it had been announced with flashy brochures loaded with propaganda and unsubstantiated claims. The guys in the Gulf didn't like it then and they didn't like it now. They had reluctantly agreed to do a pilot but made damn sure the rig they tested it on would demonstrate the new technology's utter lack of utility. I had seen that before.

Sure enough, the trial proved the technology was not cost justified on that oil platform. Then Katrina hit. The whole issue was shelved, pushed to the back burner for well over a year while other, more pressing decisions were made and while New Orleans began to recover.

But headquarters did not forget. They believed in the technology. It was already up and running in Africa. Indonesia and the North Sea were testing it on platforms, where it would do well. But the Gulf still rejected the mandate. This was the single most profitable region and they were not about to be told how to run their business. They had clout because they led in generating profit. But was it worth maintaining their independence if it meant missing the inflection point that could carry them forward or leave them behind?

The analyst from headquarters caved. "You are right. We cannot say this technology is solely responsible for those results." But he was quick to add, "In my gut I just know this is the right thing to do; this is going to change the whole industry and we have to be there, too!" The guy from the Gulf joined him, "You know, I can respect that. Let's take a closer look and see what this can do for us."

What brought them to agreement was the guy from headquarters shifting from the propaganda platform to saying that he knew *in his gut* that an inflection point was on them. Down-hole technology was changing the oil business.

I ended up taking a lead consulting position with the Americas division as they implemented the new technology. Two years later there was a futuristic room in the Gulf of Mexico's main office that looked like the bridge on Star Trek. But it was not its looks that made it innovative—it was the value it brought to operations and the hydrocarbon they took to the bank as a result. This company used the inflection point created by down-hole technology and rode it to maintain and even increase its position as the most profitable energy company in the world.

This is the story of a how one company rode an inflection point into a better future. But if you don't see an inflection point for what it is and act decisively, it can take you out of the game entirely. I have sat in rooms with leaders who just don't see them. The whole world is changing and for some reason their radar is not picking it up. I am going to show you in the pages ahead how to make sure you *never* join their ranks.

I will lay out the four types of inflection points so that you can recognize them as they are emerging. This way you will be able to see them in advance more readily and then align your offerings to best take advantage of them. You can also better prepare to drive your own positive inflection points, jetting your organization into growth mode.

Take for example the Human Resources Certification Institute (HRCI). Created as a separate organization by the Society of Human Resource Professionals in 1973, it is solely and independently responsible for developing and administering certification exams in the field of human resources.

Initially growth was slow. By 1981, under the name of the Personnel Accreditation Institute, they had certified around 2,500 human resources (HR) professionals. In 1988 they established their two mainstay certifications, the Professional in HR® and the Senior Professional in HR®. Growth was incremental, steady. But all that changed in the middle of the first decade of the 21st century when the group introduced a sequence of game-changing products and services.

The time seemed ripe. Although companies had for years been giving lip service to the idea that people are their biggest assets, the age of the knowledge economy made that a reality, and HR deserved its place on the frontier of strategic talent development. People had become the primary competitive advantage for knowledge organizations.

The inflection point was the strategic use of HR; that is, developing and acquiring the talent explicitly to drive success in the market. Globally organizations were moving from viewing HR as the birthday-benefits people to HR as the source of the leaders required for growth.

HRCI determined it would be at the forefront of this inflection point, establishing itself as the midwife of professional standards required to succeed in a global marketplace. Innovation would be their tool of choice. Here is a high-level timeline of HRCI's tactical innovations designed to drive a positive inflection point for the organization in relation to their market:

- 2004—Global Professional in HR hits the market, establishing international HR certification standards.
- 2005—The exam is taken online–worldwide, one of the first certifications conducted via the web.
- 2007—Specialized exams for the state of California are introduced.
- 2008—An online directory of approved preparation providers is launched.
- 2010—HRCI's national conversation on strategic HR is launched.
- 2011—The first symposia on strategic HR and innovation takes place in Washington, DC.
- 2012—Launch of the in-house publication, *Certified*, focusing exclusively on the intersection of HR, strategy, and innovation. National symposia are held in Washington, DC, and New York with dates for 2013 in San Francisco, Chicago, Toronto, and Seoul.

Each of these innovations combined to increase awareness of HRCI among its target clients at a time when HR was becoming more visibly crucial to business success. They demonstrated that HRCI was moving aggressively into a new role as a thought leader at the forefront of strategic HR, not just a purveyor of certifications. The global certification of 2004 was a huge step forward, providing practical guidance in a complex world of increasingly multinational organizations. The online exam was one of the first to enable applicants to test electronically, ensuring HRCI's leadership in an increasingly Internet-enabled world. And so on. Each of these accomplishments moved them forward decisively as a leader in their field.

The combined result was a reputation for being at the forefront at a time when strategic HR was a competitive advantage. The success of these efforts could be measured in certifications issued. By 2008 the count was up to about 96,000. At the time of writing, summer 2012, their certificant base had reached over 125,000 in 100 countries.[5]

This sequence of steps was intentionally designed and executed to garner a positive inflection point for the organization. You can feel the results when you walk the halls of HRCI's offices. The buzz is palpable. Leadership is on a roll. The level of productivity is off the charts, with synergies being cultivated and harvested faster than any one person can orchestrate.

HRCI is on the ascent. They are an organization to watch, appreciate, and join. They have changed the game from HR certification to HR leadership, and as a result their market success is on an upward climb. HRCI's sphere of influence is expanding to include CEOs, business leaders, and other players who understand the need for talent management as a critical component of organizational strategy and success.

HRCI's positive inflection point has resulted in a growing customer base, increased purchases as individuals choose to take more than one certification, loyalty during an economic downturn, and a real move up market, claiming and owning their niche.

Four Targets for Innovation Strategy

Recognizing and leveraging inflection points can make a real contribution to four strategic targets:

1. Growing your base
2. Getting a bigger buy
3. Improving loyalty
4. Increasing market prominence

Which of these targets best fits your current situation? Let's consider the gains that can result from aiming at each, and the tactics to do so in more detail. I will use HRCI's example to illustrate.

Growing Your Base

Expanding your customer base depends on five factors:

1. Current customer satisfaction
2. Desire for your offering
3. Your reputation as a provider
4. A value proposition you can deliver
5. Effective outreach

Any one of these factors can significantly limit or enhance the development of new customers. Done well together they create synergies that enhance, reinforce, and build upon each other's capacity to grow your base.

Current customer satisfaction describes how content today's customers are with you. The higher their satisfaction, the easier you'll find it to build the base. Satisfied customers become evangelists, provide positive reviews, and refer people to your business.

Desire for your offering is an indicator of the pull for your products and services; it tells you how much the market wants what you have and therefore how likely it is to embrace your offering.

Your reputation as a provider contributes significantly to the trust the market puts in your ability, which in turn accelerates acceptance.

A value proposition you can deliver is essential. If the other factors are in your favor, customers will give you a try, and then it's up to you to provide the goods. This is what makes your offering credible.

Effective outreach means that you are getting the attention of the people who matter; that is, you are in front of your target audience delivering messages they want to hear in media they prefer.

Bring these five factors together and you have the makings of a solid growth effort. For example, the HRCI activities rely on effective communication to a base of satisfied customers who want the value of certification and trust HRCI to deliver, with quality certification and recertification keeping certificants relevant and up to speed in an ever-changing field. Satisfied customers lend credence by recertifying, obtaining certification in more than one area, sharing their stories, attending events, and spreading the word to their peers. Each of these strengthens growth in HRCI's market and contributes power to their positive inflection point.

Getting a Bigger Buy

A bigger buy means that you are growing the amount of spend your customers are giving you, as opposed to other providers they can choose for the same services or products.

HRCI got a bigger buy from their audience by expanding the certifications they provided, making it possible for individuals to pursue more than one. Professionals in the field can expand their expertise as they rise through the ranks from Professional in Human Resources (PHR) to Senior Professional in Human Resources (SPHR). If they are operating in a global environment they can also become certified as a Global Professional in Human Resources. Those who already hold PHR and SPHR credentials and want to become expert in regulations and legal mandates specific to the state of California can earn the additional certificates, PHR-CA and SPHR-CA. In this way HRCI has increased the spend clients can give them.

There is an important nuance to growing a bigger spend. I call it *customer-centric competitive differentiation*. Here is an example to illustrate. If you are a hardware store competing with two other stores in your locale, your customers are spreading their business across three stores. Getting a bigger buy in this situation means differentiating yourself from the other two in a way that causes customers to choose you over them. Some of those you are courting are already your customers, but they go to the other two stores, too, for a variety of reasons. Your job is to figure out why and bring everyone to your store whenever possible. This is competitive differentiation.

If you are engaged in winning customers from others (that is, operating in a competitive environment), it's helpful to think of the customer base as existing in three spaces, as in Figure 1.1.

On the far left inside *Your Operation*, you see the *D-zone*, so named because this symbolizes your *dedicated* customers. These people have

Getting Innovation Right

FIGURE 1.1 Customer Spaces in a Competitive Environment

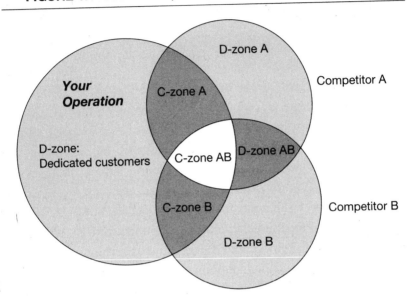

already decided that you are the provider for them. Your primary activity in this space is maintaining this group, ensuring they stay dedicated. This is your home base. There is no competition here. However, you always want to be alert to any indication your customers are migrating to one of the other six zones.

On the far right are similar D-zones. These are your competitors' home bases. *D-zone A* represents all the customers who are dedicated to doing business with Competitor A, and *D-zone B* is the same for Competitor B. *D-zone AB* indicates those customers torn between your competitors, but not considering you—in other words, they are dedicated to A or B. Since you are not in the mix, this is not an area of competition for you. *You can only compete where customers are torn between you and another.*

In the middle are the C-zones, named for *competition*. Here is where the battle rages. *C-zone A* represents those customers deciding between you and Competitor A. *C-zone B* represents those doing the same with you and Competitor B. *C-zone AB* are those wrestling between you and A or B.

The key to competition is not *just* what distinguishes you from your competitors. It is what differentiates you *in the areas your customers care about.*

For example, you may have lower prices and feel this is your unique differentiator. But customers may be looking for convenience and willing to pay more for it. If stores A and B get their customers in and out of the store in less than half the time as you, you are misplacing your resources to focus on price. Hire a few extra people to work the floor, teach your cashiers to operate with speed even if it means you have to raise your prices to pay for the extra staff. Conduct a marketing campaign to highlight how you get your customers in and out of the store more rapidly than your competitors.

It is critical that you understand what your competitors are providing *that is central to your customers.* That is the front of the battle. To gain customers from the competition you must differentiate yourself and compete here. Thus the name, customer-centric competitive differentiation.

To compete successfully you must work hard to understand what motivates potential customers to choose you over your competitors. Then you are in a position to turn their behavior. If you only focus on what you offer, you miss the actual competition zone, the front in the battle where customers are won.

Another look at our chart in Figure 1.2 and you will see the three intersection zones that overlap with *Your Operation* form "the front" of the battle. This is where you compete.

You may have customers who move from your D-zone toward your competitors. To do so they will have to cross through the front where they make their decision about who to patronize. If you are suffering an exodus you must fortify the front facing your own home base. You can do this by reinforcing what your dedicated customers value.

A positive inflection point is an excellent tool to capture the attention of your competitors' existing customers and stimulate them

FIGURE 1.2 The Front in the Battle to Win Customers

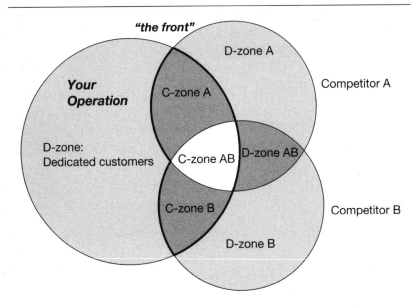

to make a decision about who they are going to buy from, thus moving them into the front where they become available to you.

When Verizon launched FIOS, their bundle of home communications services, they created an inflection point by bringing fiber optics straight to the homes of their customers. This grabbed the attention of many who went on to reevaluate their service providers and decided to leave Comcast and other competitors to experience fiber optics at home. By so doing Verizon moved competitors' customers out of their opponents' dedication zones and onto the front where many were then acquired. Then Verizon was in a position to get a bigger buy by bundling services, which they did.

Improving Loyalty

One of the biggest market challenges in recent decades was the 2008 economic downturn. Many leaders found holding onto their client base exceptionally hard. Any weakness in customer relationship became stark as portfolios shrank and customers took a hard look at their spending.

What became apparent all too quickly in this dire market was how many organizations were suffering from one of these three unfortunate circumstances:

- Offerings were no longer competitive. Customers were able to get sufficient quality or, in some instances, better for less cost elsewhere.
- Customer care became disconnected from value. In essence, customer care became a nice-to-have, not a must-have. When times were hard, it was exchanged by the customers for cost savings where possible. This means that customers were quick to jump to another provider even when customer care was clearly worse, as long as there were financial rewards.
- Customers were in trouble themselves, slashing their expenses severely and sometimes indiscriminately. They made loyalty decisions poorly, but made them nonetheless.

Creating an inflection point in this environment is an excellent solution that revives loyalty and holds onto your existing base. It can reorient the customers' mind-set from surviving to thriving. If customers believe that by sticking with you they will be able to get through the downturn successfully, their loyalty increases. They become more willing to tolerate challenges buoyed by the hope of a better future.

For example, HRCI increased loyalty at a time when others were losing it by establishing their presence as a thought leader in strategic HR during the economic downturn of 2008. They associated their certifications with job success. It was a way out of dismal prospects in the minds of their customers. Certification is both a job security tactic and a job-seeking strategy. It became necessary in an environment riddled with job loss and the resulting uncertainty, a buffer against difficult circumstances.

By embracing a downturn and associating yourself with a way out, rather than avoiding or hunkering down to weather the storm, you can reverse the trend of disloyalty and increase steadfast dedication among your customers.

Increasing Market Prominence

When Avis, second to Hertz, adopted their slogan, *We try harder*, they were not even making a profit. Within three years under the banner of that slogan they became a credible force in the industry, a position they continue to hold to this day. They increased their prominence in the market by carving out a space that they *were* first in. They put in *more* effort, took their role *more* seriously than Hertz — or so they claimed. The innovation in this case was making #2 the place to be in the customers' minds instead of #1. The inflection point was positioning customer service as the defining value rather than market domination. With success riding on customer service, Avis moved from unprofitability to solvency while growing their market share from 11% in 1962 to 35% in 1966.[6]

You need not be first in what appears to be your niche (for Avis it was rental cars), but you must be first in something. Only then can you attract new customers, build your base, extend your profits, and move up market.

HRCI shifted their position out from under their progenitor's shadow to create a center of gravity all their own, establishing a global brand and attracting new clientele through their reputation as the thought leader for strategic HR. They increased their market prominence significantly by using their inflection point to secure their position as global leader in HR certification.

Now that we have looked at the four targets of inflection points, let's take a deeper look at what exactly an inflection point is, the different types of inflection points both negative and positive so you can recognize and discover them, and how multiple inflection points can be combined to generate a Turnaround.

Inflection Points Defined

HRCI leads today in supporting HR practitioners worldwide, lifting them out of the ranks through certification, and facilitating a national conversation on strategy, innovation, leadership, and the contribution of HR to succeeding in business. As a result of a positive inflection point, they changed their game and garnered market favor. That's how organizations get ahead, move out in front of others, reposition themselves as leaders, and claim ownership of their niche.

My use of the term *inflection point* borrows from both mathematics and economics but is a generalization not bound by the rules of either. I use the term to highlight an important business dynamic, a game change that shifts circumstances forcefully. I am talking about *a decisive change in the status of your organization with respect to its success in the market.* This is not an independent phenomenon, but an event that takes place between you and the market. It can be either negative, indicating a drop, or positive, demonstrating market success.

I illustrate with graphs that depict an organization's path through its inflection point. For these illustrations, time is always moving us forward into the future, left to right. The vertical axis shows how the organization is doing in the market: up means success is on the rise and down means it is in decline.

First I go through the negative inflection points (diagrammed in Figure 1.3) that show a turn for the worse. Each of these reflects a game

FIGURE 1.3 Negative Inflection Points

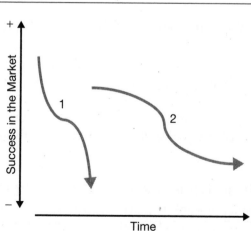

FIGURE 1.4 Positive Inflection Points

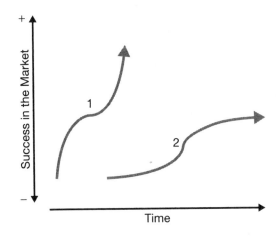

change that shifts circumstances decisively against you: a trajectory to avoid.

Then I discuss the positive inflection points (shown in Figure 1.4), highlighting a variety of increases in market success; that is, game changes that shift circumstances decisively in your favor. These, of course, are the inflection points we pursue and leverage.

Negative Inflection Points

There are two types of negative inflection points:

1. *Vertical Drop*: A downward fall levels and then falls again, this time decisively.
2. *Step Down*: A shallow descent drops precipitously and then levels out in shallow but ongoing decline.

While we strive for positive turns, it is good to have a thorough understanding of the negative. Business, like life, is filled with its fair share of both.

Vertical Drop: This is what happens when an organization is on its way down and is not able to pull out and achieve a Turnaround. The inflection point here portends demise. Success in the market is on a downward slope to begin with, but it starts to flatten out before taking a turn for the worse. Then performance plummets.

We see this kind of behavior when a leader makes a bad move just as the drop in market success is starting to slow, or other factors move in to impact an already-weak situation and seal its doom.

The way out of this is to go for a Turnaround, a tactic I detail later in this chapter.

Step Down: Although this is a less-than-ideal scenario, it does not end in death. Instead the organization plateaus at a lower level of success than it began. This is preferable to annihilation and can be engineered into a Turnaround somewhat more easily than a Vertical Drop.

Here you have an organization that was on its way down, too — see the shallow descent turning steep at the midway point in the second curve in Figure 1.3. The inflection point actually reorients the path so that it is heading off to the right rather than on to the bottom. This means that some form of stability has staved off a nosedive and resulting obliteration. The stability is very important to understand, as it is likely to be a primary asset in putting together a Turnaround.

While the way out of both the Vertical Drop and the Step Down is a Turnaround, a Vertical Drop has greater downward momentum and is thus more difficult to shift in direction. As a result, it is almost always easier to first shift a Vertical Drop into a Step Down and then shift the resulting Step Down into a positive inflection point.

For example, if your company is in a free fall, out of market favor, and losing customers quickly, you may find a way to hold onto a certain segment and be able to do so even if you cannot pull the organization into a climb right away. Securing a segment of your customers moves you from the Vertical Drop into a Step Down. Then you can work with that segment to shift to a rise in market prominence. By viewing the Turnaround process in two steps, it becomes easier to see the action steps that lead to your desired result, market success.

Now that we have seen the inflection points that spell trouble, let's move to those we all desire: inflection points that signal market success.

Positive Inflection Points

The two types of positive inflection points are

1. *Vertical Climb*: A steep climb shifts to a plateau then a near vertical ascent.
2. *Step Up*: A shallow ascent accelerates up and then levels out as a plateau.

Vertical Climb: Here is an organization that was on its way up, began to level out, and then shifted to an ascent. We see (from the zoom view in Figure 1.5) that the curve is heading off to the right in a plateau before it begins to ascend dramatically.

This pattern is typical of many organizations today. After a strong run it is considered normal to flatten out, even decline. The traditional innovation S-curves (portrayed in Figure 1.6) suggest the need for a sequence of innovations to avoid plateaus and achieve continuous growth.

This is effective. But it is much more powerful when an inflection point takes place that fundamentally shifts circumstances in your favor. This requires not a linear sequence of innovations, but a multipronged approach that includes building capacity, generating value, turning

FIGURE 1.5 The Vertical Climb

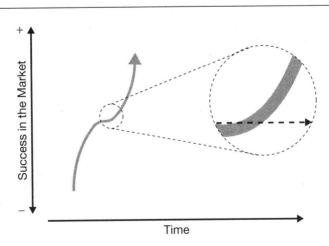

FIGURE 1.6 Traditional Innovation S-Curves

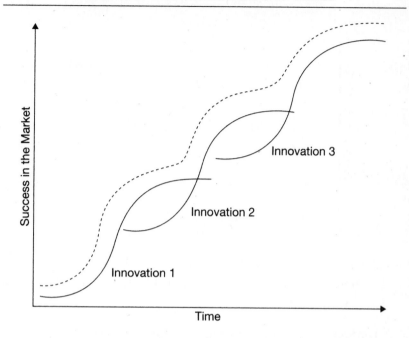

disruption to your advantage, and engaging your target customers for best possible delivery. All of these are covered in detail in the chapters ahead.

The end of the Vertical Climb's curve points almost straight up rather than at the flatter angle of the Step Up. Through this type of inflection point you shift market success through a plateau into the aggressive climb of dramatic growth.

Step Up: Here (in Figure 1.7) we see a curve moving from an upward tilting plateau through an ascent into another plateau.

Why would we want to stabilize rather than continue up? There are three good reasons:

1. Resources are exhausted. You need to secure position and refuel.
2. Timing is not right for the next level of growth. You need to reassess, bring in different talent, or wait for the opportunity window to open to mount the next stage of growth.

FIGURE 1.7 The Step Up

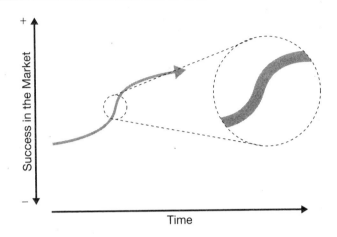

3. You have achieved your target and now need to dedicate resources to other activity; for example, engaging the increased base you now have exposure to.

The Step Up is particularly effective when you have tapped a source of value that can provide an ongoing stream of profitable customers but is pulling you in directions you don't want to go. Let me give an example to illustrate.

Roger Scheumann and Carolyn Weinberg, owners of Quartermaine Coffee Roasters, started out as Peet's Coffee & Tea protégés. I met them after I wrote my first book in their coffee shop. It's a great place to get locally brewed coffee and write in Bethesda, Maryland.

When Peet's Coffee & Tea decided to close down the Quartermaine brand Roger and Carolyn bought it. Their hard work produced seven stores and a wholesale business that included an account with Walmart. By all accounts they were well on their way.

Then they created something new that propelled them into success rapidly. Working with local restaurant, Clyde's Restaurant Group, Roger and Carolyn developed a customized roast, *Clyde's blend*, that achieved great success among customers. But the wait staff did not always make a great cup of coffee, so Roger and Carolyn developed a training program to ensure that every cup was uniformly excellent, a monitoring process that made it possible for Clyde's Restaurant Group executives to detect how well their employees adhered to the procedures and a course correction methodology that could be applied as needed to ensure customers were getting the coffee experience they wanted. This quality control system, predicated on a quality coffee experience for customers, was the innovation that launched them into a whole new level of success.

Their innovation required them to install and maintain the coffee machines, train employees, develop and gather metrics, report to management, and support employees when coffee quality went down. The result was a powerful coffee experience that grew their brand so well demand moved first from restaurant to local stores. As a result of the popularity a very large chain picked up the coffee. Their innovation had springboarded them from local roaster to national phenomenon. They had created a Vertical Climb inflection point.

But Roger and Carolyn did not want to grow, grow, and grow. They wanted a business lifestyle that matched their desire for fun, family, and other pursuits. They closed down all the retails shops except for one that was within easy driving distance of their homes. They sold the coffee wholesale, but let go of managing the stores. They concentrated on their roasting facility, one retail shop, and building relationships with local restaurants where the taste of their coffee was central.

Then they received an offer for a second location. It was close to their homes but a different culture altogether from their one successful store. Not being in the heart of a small city like Bethesda, they would have to adapt to a new clientele. After some examination they decided the new location fit their criteria and they decided to go forward.

Business didn't come easy the first year. The landlord didn't understand their style. The mall they were in had not had a community coffee shop. They had to find innovative ways to attract the locals. As of this writing they are in their second year at the new location and things are going well, but they are not pursuing additional growth. Instead they are stabilizing, creating a Step Up inflection point. They are working to lock in their success rather than secure new ground.

Using Inflection Points to Create Success

When you begin to pursue inflection points, you start to look at the world in a different way. Jeff Bezos sensed an inflection point when he learned about the rapid growth in Internet use through his job in a hedge fund.[7] He determined to get ahead of the curve and put together a business plan, incorporated in 1994, and turned his first profit in the fourth quarter of 2001.[8] It took him seven years of aggressive driving to achieve the inflection point that buoyed Amazon.com to its current position.

With his knowledge of the coming changes in technology he was able to brave years of investor losses and steer successfully toward the day when it would all turn around and he would achieve a positive inflection point, a dramatic and decisive rise in success in his market. Today, the business he founded, Amazon.com, is the most profitable online retailer in the world.[9]

Pursuing inflection points requires attention to market movements, a clear understanding of emerging opportunities and challenges, the ability to question basic assumptions, and skill at turning disruption to your advantage. All of these are covered in the chapters ahead in detail. But once you understand the opportunities that circumstances are giving rise to, how do you position yourself to harness those conditions favorably?

Three Inflection Point Tactics

There are several basic tactics that can be used to take advantage of changing market conditions. They can be executed independently or combined to create more complex responses such as a Turnaround. The three that I will elaborate on here are

1. Stop the Drop
2. Shift to Ascent
3. Soar

Inflection point tactics are simple moves that change your relationship to an upward or downward trend. Each tactic is designed to accelerate or stabilize your success in the market.

Stop the Drop: This tactic, shown in Figure 1.8, is one of the most important to learn, as it rescues you from impending disaster. It takes a situation in rapid decline and creates a plateau to stop the downturn. It is the first stage of a Turnaround, covered in more detail after the three tactics.

When an organization is in free fall something dramatic is called for to stop the nosedive.

One of my CEO clients was in command of an old-school organization that served an industry experiencing a significant transition, gasoline station owners. He was on top of his numbers and knew his profits were declining and leading him into the red.

The longstanding customers were all white males who believed knowledge-sharing was what you do at the bar after work with your best buddies. As they retired and left his organization, his numbers went down. The new clients were Asian, African American, and Hispanic, including women as well as men. Many were young, some just out of college, with others even younger, helping their families run operations.

The new crowd appreciated an online approach. Many were immigrants and worked long hours. Their culture was such that they would

FIGURE 1.8 Stop the Drop

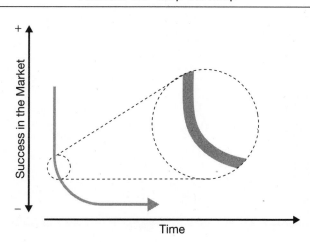

not take time out to get away from work. However, they were very interested in learning from others.

My client created a migration path from traditional strategies that included annual meetings that were thinly disguised pleasure trips. He moved his organization to a suite of online communities that could be accessed 24/7 from anywhere there was an Internet connection.

He did a rigorous accounting of the costs and revenues he had to generate and intentionally took his organization from one mode of operation to the other. By shifting decisively away from leading the old boy's club and toward real value delivery online he stopped the drop.

Shift to Ascent: Aggressive growth is not always the aim, even when growth is sought. Sometimes establishing a slow growth presence in the market is desired. This tactic (shown in Figure 1.9) yields a gentle incline as an outcome.

Slow growth can be good if infrastructure is an issue. Often it is the case that a firm will use an investment to grow. If that growth takes off, the original investment may not be enough to build the infrastructure required to ensure the quality necessary for continued, rapid growth. If quality goes down as speed of growth goes up, sustainability is sacrificed.

FIGURE 1.9 Shift to Ascent

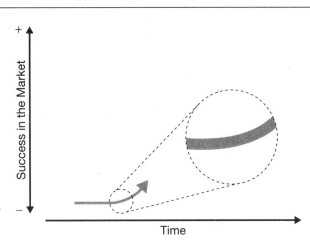

You may even build up animosity in the market that will sabotage your growth.

Another instance when slow growth can be helpful is when issues of scale arise. Sometimes a business model that works very well at one scale has challenges associated with speedy growth. For example 'wichcraft, the New York, Las Vegas, and San Francisco sandwich shop that built its reputation on fresh ingredients, has taken its time growing its first 14 locations. This was necessary so they could work out the supply chain required to make the small batches of fresh preparations responsible for their success.[10]

Soar: This tactic, shown in Figure 1.10, shifts you from steady to dramatic growth. The organization is already on the way up when its success moves to another level, creating a Vertical Climb. This is a demanding transition, requiring excellence in execution to sustain. Although it appears at first glance to be a desired state, many are not prepared for the activity required to sustain it.

A primary area of concern is infrastructure. Your infrastructure must be ready to handle a large spike in activity to achieve a Soar inflection point. An example of success in this regard is Animoto.com, a web-based video producer.

FIGURE 1.10 Soar

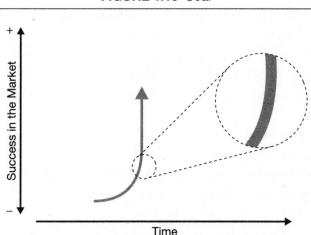

The Animoto site will take photos, video, music, and sound files, and combine them into a short video you can download and share with your friends. It's a creative way to generate home movies and works for business presentations, too.

Animoto launched in 2007 and was received well, attracting funding and users at a significant pace. In 2008 they launched an application on Facebook and experienced a huge spike in new users, resulting in a need for massive computing power fast.

They went from 25,000 customers to 750,000 in four days. To process all the registrations and videos they required the use of up to 5,000 servers simultaneously.[11] Brad Jefferson, one of the founders, said, "Without the ability to handle a spike like that, our business doesn't exist."[12]

Animoto did it using cloud computing purchased from Amazon. As their need increased Amazon was able to dedicate the resources, and as their need diminished Amazon followed along, hugging demand closely.

This type of arrangement makes it possible for companies working with cloud providers to experience huge spikes in computing power, both the climb and the drop, without sacrificing customer experience. Further, the close matching by Amazon ensures they stay in the black, never spending more than they need.

Not so long ago a company like Animoto would have had to buy servers, the facility to house them, and the staff to run them in advance. A huge expense like this is not justified unless a big increase in revenue is clearly coming. This is often something no one can predict accurately. And when the spike is over, what do you do with the servers, facility, and people?

The process of powering down, so to speak, has tremendous overhead. But with the advent of cloud computing all that changes for the better, enabling companies like Animoto to pull off the Soar tactic while they maximize their profits in the process.

Each of these three tactics is easier to talk about than to execute. These simple moves take an extraordinary amount of skill. Now that you have an understanding of what they are, I will show you how they can be combined to create a more complex move, the Turnaround.

The Turnaround

The Turnaround (illustrated in Figure 1.11) is one of the most difficult maneuvers to manage, yet it is also one of the most important and lucrative when done successfully. As a result there are leaders who specialize in it.

A Turnaround delivers three inflection points sequentially: (a) Stop the Drop, (b) Shift to Ascent, then (c) Soar. Each requires its own effort.

First you have to pull out of your nosedive, Stop the Drop. This is all about steering the organization away from doom. It typically involves changing staff, implementing new and better systems, getting reliable data, and sometimes slashing expenses beyond what can be sustained in operations; for example, temporary salary cuts. The result is a stabilization or plateau. Typically that alone does not improve your standing in the market. Instead it stabilizes the organization, averting a nasty ending. But you cannot cut your way to success—and so there is more to do.

Once you are no longer drowning, just treading water, you shift to improving your market standing. The focus is less on cutting

FIGURE 1.11 Turnaround

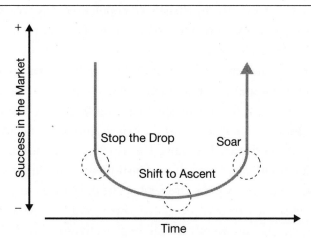

expenses and more on generating enough revenue for operations while establishing solid value for your customer base. You begin to earn your keep. This is the Shift to Ascent.

Finally, you put the pieces in place to take off with an eye toward success. All the changes you have instituted are now put to the test: great staff, robust systems, rigorous financials, market aggression, and partnerships. If successful you Soar, and you are not only back in business, you are on your way to the top. I will share a story so you will see the exceptional leadership necessary to execute this kind of dramatic change.

I serve on the board of the Columbia Lighthouse for the Blind (CLB), a Washington, DC, nonprofit, and was privy to their recent Turnaround from the inside, providing strategy to CEO Tony Cancelosi pro bono. I read the financial statements before and after. I watched Cancelosi operate on multiple fronts to pull the organization out of a nosedive and get it back in the community as a rising star.

Founded in 1900, CLB enables people of all ages who are blind, visually impaired, and deaf-blind to remain independent, active, and productive in society. Their programs and services include training and consultation in assistive technology, employment marketing, skills training, career placement services, comprehensive low-vision care, and a wide range of counseling and rehabilitation services. While their mission is to help the visually challenged population of the Washington, DC, metro region, they provide assistive technology and training in 83 cities across the United States.

But in 2005 the century-plus-old CLB was going down, an outdated institution in the red and plummeting fast. That year Cancelosi was hired as CEO to get the organization back on track. The first thing he did when he arrived was to review the bylaws, turn over the board, and implement solid financial systems. He also reviewed and turned over staff, took a cut in salary himself, and instituted a short furlough. All of this was intended to Stop the Drop, which he did successfully.

Cancelosi then focused on reinvigorating CLB's presence in the Washington, DC, community by building an advisory board of movers and shakers, combining veteran business leaders with up-and-coming firebrands. Simultaneously he focused efforts on improving services to the visually impaired and instituting innovations to resuscitate the ailing organization. Central to his efforts is the program Bridge to Work, training for wounded warriors. Bridge to Work ensures that veterans who are blind or visually impaired have the skills, resources, and training they need to succeed in the workplace. It does this by giving them training in digital data scanning, computer skills, and job interviewing.

"The disabilities groups within the different counties recognized the fact that our veterans were coming back through miracle medical attention and had all the capabilities of survival," he said to me. "Yet they still needed to be reconstituted back into society at a level that they could be earning a living and maintain the quality of life they had before they went into the military."

Cancelosi envisioned an innovation. He wanted not only to train the veterans in skills they could market and use to gain employment. He wanted to match them with jobs. He wanted to provide a complete end-to-end solution, one that started with the veteran's desire to reenter the workforce and ended with secure employment. Cancelosi used CLB as an incubator to test the Bridge to Work program.

After three years and cross-county support, he built a mature program and began identifying corporate sponsors. This program, along with others that Cancelosi has put together, is now responsible for government funding that has taken the Lighthouse to a whole new level of operation. He successfully engineered a Shift to Ascent.

In 2011 CLB put on their first Light the Way 5k run. The goal of the run was to increase public awareness of CLB's work restoring independence to the visually impaired and open the way to new partnerships that would amplify CLB's success. Through media coverage and public participation he wanted people to learn how CLB was making a difference.

Cancelosi recruited Charlie Plaskon to be spokesperson for the Light the Way 5k. Since 2003 Plaskon has completed eight half Ironman events, six full Ironman events, including the World Championship in Kona, Hawaii in October, 2007. He has six Olympic distance triathlons to his credit including the ITU World Championship representing the United States as part of Team USA in Lausanne, Switzerland in 2006. He has been featured in two Ironman documentaries carried nationally on NBC and the Outdoor Life Network. Charlie is in his late 60s and blind.

Cancelosi brought Plaskon in not just to speak about the Light the Way 5k, but to run and teach other participants how to lead runners who are visually impaired. This way the visually impaired could participate and everyone who was up for the challenge had the chance to be a guide.

The event netted $80,000, far more than most 5ks garner their first year. More importantly it established partnerships in the community that included the Washington Nationals and Safeway. It did this by involving the key members of their staff in the race as sponsors and participants. Steve Neibergall, president of Safeway's Eastern Division and veteran marathoner, left me in his dust as I ran the course.

Once people experienced what CLB was all about firsthand, they wanted to deepen their involvement. The same year as the first race Cancelosi began a professional fundraising campaign and received several significant estate donations.

He poured energy into his grant acquisition program and garnered millions of dollars in multiyear contracts from the federal government, including the Federal Bureau of Investigation, Internal Revenue Service, Department of Veterans Affairs, Andrews Air Force Base, and the Department of Education. Many smaller grants were also acquired. He opened relationships with the Workforce Investment Boards of three local counties and the District of Columbia.

In 2011 not only was CLB in the black, it was garnering media attention and new major partnerships. All of these efforts were parlayed back into core services improving the quality of care to help the visually impaired achieve independence. As of 2012 Cancelosi is in the early stages of a Soar. CLB is no longer known as an old-school charity. It is now a savvy business partner attracting top-level sponsors in the Washington, DC, community.

With emotional intensity Cancelosi executed each of the three tactics that together generated a Turnaround. His is a perfect example of how to combine basic moves for a more sophisticated result.

The overarching innovation Cancelosi brought to CLB was his ability to run it like a business. Every step of the way his tactics were engineered to lift the numbers. He ran the nonprofit with the rigor of a business perspective. He never compromised on CLB's core mission. But he pulled every lever at his disposal as a CEO, from salaries to systems, from marketing to partnerships, to move CLB from the red to the black.

Seeing Around the Curve

Inflection points are important because they enable decisive shifts in market acceptance. Being able to sense them in advance and prepare your organization to take advantage of them positions you for innovations that will succeed in the market—the only kind that really matter.

Looking for inflection points and detecting them in advance positions you to win big in important areas. Without developing this sense, you will find it extremely difficult to get innovation right. Increasing your ability to find inflection points and applying the tactics to turn them to your advantage will help you grow your base, get a bigger buy from existing customers, improve loyalty even in tough times, and increase market prominence.

Every one of the chapters that follows teaches skills that will help you discover inflection points and take advantage of them when you spot them coming.

EXPERT INPUT: CINDY HALLBERLIN OF GOOD360.ORG ON GETTING AHEAD OF AN INFLECTION POINT

Cindy Hallberlin, CEO of Good360.org, is a dynamo with a mission. She has a history of successfully tackling really tough business challenges. As the chief ethics and compliance officer following a $1 billion fraud, she oversaw the cultural transformation of US Foodservice.

Expert Input

Before that she developed and successfully managed the US Postal Service's REDRESS employment mediation program, which successfully resolved more than 80% of discrimination claims and resulted in $60 million in cost avoidance.

An international nonprofit with nearly 30 years of experience in product philanthropy, Good360 is dedicated to helping people and communities in need by distributing corporate product donations to qualified nonprofits. On behalf of Fortune 500 consumer, retail, and technology companies, Good360 distributes products to a network of more than 30,000 prevetted organizations and is consistently ranked by Forbes as one of the top 10 most efficient charities in America.[13]

Good360 has delivered more than $7 billion of donated products to tens of thousands of nonprofits and schools. Every Good360-registered nonprofit can access their online catalog to browse products donated by America's top brands such as The Home Depot, 3M, Hallmark, Bed Bath & Beyond, Crayola, Sears, Walmart, Life Is Good, and many others. Registration is free and all a nonprofit needs is proof of their organization's 501(c)(3) status, an active Form 990 provided to the IRS or financial documentation that demonstrates how programs are funded, and a signed Good360 Product Use Guidelines agreement.

The inflection point Hallberlin wanted to get ahead of was that of companies participating in product giving on a significant scale. It had already been established that product giving could be used as a brand element, helping a company to project an image of social responsibility. It became clear that scaling product giving would require a stronger and clearer financial case. Hallberlin's job was not just establishing the cost returns, but also ensuring Good360 was well known as the leaders in product philanthropy.

When it comes to companies unloading product, we have learned that donating not only provides scalable impact to communities in need, but can also yield a better return on investment than liquidating or disposing. This fact cannot be ignored. Strategic donation efforts — benefiting the triple bottom line (people, planet, profit) — were an inflection point in the private sector I wanted to get ahead of and steer. The way that recycling has become a social movement over the last decade, we want to lock in and seal the donation mind-set by publicizing the business case and simplifying the donation process.

To get ahead of the product giving inflection point, we knew we had to do more than connect those who have with those who need—we had to become thought leaders. We commissioned Indiana University research that was released in January 2012 showing donation to be the best financial choice over liquidation or disposal. *The Business Case for Product Philanthropy*, by economist Justin Ross, includes two worksheets companies can use to determine for themselves (1) Cost-Benefit Analysis of Liquidate, Dispose, or Donate, and (2) Return on Investment.

Our vision also demands constant innovation and it was imperative that we leverage the latest technology to stay ahead of the curve. For the product giving movement to truly catch on, we knew it had to be simple, manageable and customizable. We have the ability to tailor a giving program to fit any company's needs and strategies—from innovative employee giving programs to one-time donations to ongoing national retail initiatives.

A good example of an employee giving program is the one we developed and manage with Hewlett-Packard (HP). We set up their giving website, manage the back end, and oversee all logistical aspects. Employees are able to select HP products they want to donate through an online website, donate 25% of the cost (HP picks up the remaining 75%), and hand select which charity will receive their gift. When employees are asking more from their employers than ever before, HP provides a fantastic benefit that not only empowers employees to give back to the community, but allows selected nonprofits to receive new technology to aid their missions.

In June of 2012, the Committee Encouraging Corporate Philanthropy (CECP) honored Good360 with its Directors' Award as part of the organization's 12th Annual Excellence Awards in Corporate Philanthropy, for our exemplary partnership with The Home Depot

Expert Input

on the Framing Hope Product Donation Program. Framing Hope was created in 2008 out of The Home Depot associates' desire to donate marked-down inventory, buy-backs, returned merchandise, and end-of-season items rather than shipping them back to distribution centers or placed in landfills. By partnering with Good360 to manage all aspects of the program, The Home Depot was able to distribute more than $100M in products to more than 1,000 prequalified nonprofits across the country.

Influencing a powerful trend like corporate giving on a large scale is a real challenge. Operations are massive and complex. But a keen eye for Good360's inflection point indicated what was needed: (1) a strong financial case she could present to her customers, (2) easy-to-use tools her customers' CFOs can apply to their organizations, (3) highly customizable and easy-to-implement employee participation programs, and (4) a reputation for thought leadership in the field demonstrating that Good360 is the partner of choice. These are the tools Hallberlin plied to successfully achieve her positive inflection point.

Success Rules

- Create inflection points that drive you toward one or more of four targets:
  1. Growing your base
  2. Getting a bigger buy
  3. Improving loyalty
  4. Increasing market prominence
- Growing your base depends on five primary contributing factors:
  1. Current customer satisfaction
  2. Desire for your offering
  3. Your reputation as a provider
  4. A value proposition you can deliver
  5. Effective outreach

- To get the bigger buy, exploit inflection points that bring opponents' customers into the competition-zone where they will decide who they want to engage.
- Improving loyalty requires creating an inflection point that reorients customers' mind-sets.
- To increase market prominence, carve out a space you can be first in.
- Inflection points, which can be negative or positive, and precipitous or moderate, represent a change in the status of the organization with respect to its success in the market.
- Inflection point tactics are simple moves that stabilize or accelerate your success in the market. Combine the Stop the Drop, Shift to Ascent, and Soar inflection point tactics to create a Turnaround.

Build Innovation
Capacity

If you want to systematically deliver innovations that culminate in inflection points, you cannot ignore your innovation capacity. By capacity I mean the capabilities required to channel the pressures inherent in innovation into productive use. Without this, your highest hopes, years of work, and millions of dollars can be reduced to a cloud of dirt and debris so fast you won't know what happened.

There are underpinnings you can put in place that will simultaneously keep you from failure and put you in a position to excel—specifically, leadership, talent management, and idea management. I think of these as the *innovation foundation*. If you build a foundation of strong leadership, exceptional talent management, and robust idea management into your organization, you will have the capacity to manage critical forces, containing and using the pressures that arise to advance your innovation initiatives.

I will explain these foundational elements in more detail. But first, let me introduce you to some of innovation's enemies.

Three Forces That Jeopardize Innovation

To support the difficulties of taking an innovation successfully to market, you need to build your capacity to handle the stresses and strains that innovation will inevitably cause. These three forces will jeopardize your innovation efforts:

1. The pressures of everyday operations;
2. The movement and stress that comes with new ideas, products, and services
3. Market forces: sometimes rapid, always unpredictable.

These stresses come with the territory of innovation. They cannot be stopped, circumvented, or avoided. Rather than fight them, you must meet and use them to your advantage. Meet them well, and your organization will have the capacity required to succeed at innovation. Meet them poorly, and your efforts will regularly fail.

Operational Pressures

The priority of your organization is and will always be taking care of business. This is how you deliver on your mission, keep your doors open, and make a profit. These activities unto themselves generate certain pressures. That's a part of life. The pressures include being responsive to customer demands, adapting to new policies and laws, managing cash flow, and dealing effectively with inventory, staffing issues, and many other challenges that come with running a business.

Innovation is bound to run at cross purposes with operational pressures. The two activities have different needs. Operations requires consistency and efficiency. Innovation often is irregular and can be inefficient to manage.

If managers ever have to choose between operations and innovation, they will always pick operations . . . as they should! Keeping business going always trumps new directions. So the trick is to set up operations and innovation so they do not interfere with each other.

I was able to avert a potential conflict between innovation and operational pressures when I was called in to help a stellar national sales team improve their performance. The team was responsible for billions of dollars in pension sales. After my initial interviews of the 25 members of the team and their managers it was clear there was a huge disparity across the force. Four members of the team consistently closed the vast majority of the deals. The lowest on the totem pole were closing deals that generated tens of millions of dollars in a given year. While impressive, this was a fraction of the deals their superstar counterparts closed.

We wanted the superstars to impart their knowledge to the rest of the sales force. But, they were less than cooperative. It's not that they were against sharing per se — just uninterested in any activity that took time away from their highest-value pursuit — sales.

Based on suggestions from the team we decided to create an internally-run learning event. This was a workshop run by the sales team for the sales team that would allow everyone to benefit from learning the superstars' best practices and techniques.

At first mention of the idea several of their managers rolled their eyes. What they were saying was, "This will be a waste of time. It does not compare to doing what needs to be done: more sales." As originally proposed, the learning event would span a day, taking everyone away from selling for at least eight hours plus travel time.

To be responsive to this discomfort we rolled the learning event into the regularly scheduled mandatory annual meeting already on everyone's calendar. The managers relaxed. Even though the time was easily justified on a national scale because the impact would improve team sales, it was impossible to justify at the local level for the highest performers. The time they spent teaching others was time they could have spent with customers. We moved the innovation activity, the learning event, to a position on the calendar where it did not take extra time away from operations, day-to-day sales activity. Once we did that, all was good. Both went on unimpeded. But the training would never have happened if it had to compete with sales time in the field.

If your people are telling you they don't have time for innovation because there is "real work" to be done, they are telling you that innovation and their jobs are competing with each other. That's bad news because their jobs will always win.

A solid foundation ensures that you have the capacity for innovation, which often demands time, attention, and energy from the same people who are responsible for operations. It should never come into conflict with mission-critical activities. A primary function of a proper foundation is to ensure business goes on *and* new growth is pursued, each without compromising the other.

Innovation Stress

With innovation comes stress. Although necessary for sustainable growth and profit, innovation is by definition not business-as-usual. When it courses through your organization it demands attention and creates counter-forces that can wreak havoc among those seeking to uphold the status quo.

Expanding upon existing programs, products, and services to increase and improve their value for your customers will put stress on your staff and your partners. It means they have to look at their work in new ways, let go of tried and true formulae to create and take on different tasks, and look for unfamiliar results. Successful innovation changes routines and rituals. This is stressful for those whose work is being changed. Not everyone takes kindly to having to change their way of seeing or doing things, or to changes in their job description. Even those who want to change experience stress. They may have more enthusiasm, but they, too, feel the pressures that come with innovation.

Because innovation often requires results to be measured in new ways, you have to stay ahead of current metrics and expectations. Sometimes you will be called to the front lines of innovation, working with customers while value is still being uncovered. The ways you work may have to change. This will have to be communicated back to management for successful adaptation and integration. Here is an example where I experienced this first hand.

While at the World Bank I taught hundreds of people across the organization how to use a new tool called the Task Managers Workstation. It allowed every staff member to query systems that had earlier been confined to specialists. Within a short span of months all the data was available to vice presidents, project managers, subject matter experts, economists, and support staff around the world. They began discovering new uses for the information. I was part of the implementation team. We had our hands full responding to requests, trouble-shooting issues, and providing training to all kinds of teams who were eager to put the intelligence to work.

The Task Managers Workstation was a major innovation inside the World Bank, providing unmatched access to time-series data and detailed budget, procurement, loan disbursement, and project supervision information. Its release generated creative bursts of activity. New knowledge and insights fueled ingenuity. Everyone on our team, from the developers to the trainers, found themselves caught up in the new capabilities that were being developed across the organization.

This put significant strain not just on our group but also on the people who owned the various systems. As their data became available, gaps and misinformation also became visible. Issues in data management shone brightly. Pressures emerged to fix the systems, cleanse the data, and address faulty business processes.

The situation was managed well, but there were times when pressures seemed overwhelming and people resented the increased visibility generated by the Task Managers Workstation. Keeping the trains running on time, as they say, sometimes seemed at odds with providing new functionality people were asking for.

Those using the system soon developed new products. Project teams were creating new reports. Economists were building new tables. Vice presidents identified valuable new indicators and mandated the development of dashboards so they could see them at a glance. This put stress on the owners of the respective systems. Some did well with that demand and others did not. Some saw it as the successful evolution of the value they provided. Others viewed it as an intrusion.

Organizations that successfully innovate anticipate these pressures. They know there will be a corresponding resource draw. They prepare accordingly, building the capacity before commencing the actual work of innovation. If they do not, resistance emerges from everywhere and can quickly quash the value of that innovation.

In the unfortunate environment where innovation interrupts people willy-nilly in their day-to-day work, some people challenge and argue against new ideas for the wrong reasons. Instead of evaluating innovations based on their contribution to the organization's goals, they reject the innovations because they are an intrusion in their defined responsibilities. Their arguments are compelling. Yet they are handicapping and destroying innovation.

The way around this is to build a workplace in which innovation is embraced. The spirit of growth and the inevitable changes it brings must be more than tolerated. It must be recognized as a good thing, a source of increased value and long-term sustainability.

This is not done with mantras or top-down mandates. Instead it is handled in real time by raising and lowering stress ad hoc. Think of stress as a continuum (shown in Figure 2.1). In the center is the productive stress zone, where people are creatively adapting to challenges. Above this band is the high stress zone. If stress gets to this level it causes people to freak out or lock up. Below productive stress is the low stress zone. Here complacency takes over.

Adjustments must be made as needed to keep people on their toes, inspired, and resourceful. When stress gets too high, turn it down by providing more structure. When stress drops too low, turn it up by increasing the challenge. The optimum is to keep innovation stress in the productive zone. There it will act as a constructive catalyst and help generate the solutions needed.

FIGURE 2.1 Stress Zones

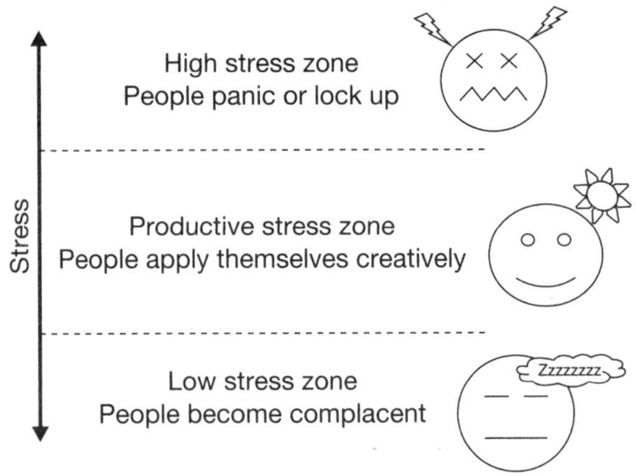

Changing Market Forces

Every business owner knows the market can shift on a dime or a headline. Positive inflection points are sometimes generated in response to these changes in market conditions. For innovation to thrive, you must have the capacity to provide both the stability required to weather change and the flexibility to jump at sudden advantage.

Here is an example of an organization that was able to respond productively in time to generate a major revenue stream when the opportunity presented itself. In 2010 I spoke with an executive vice president of a Fortune 5 company who told me about a radical opportunity he was able to capture. He ran an international division focused on hardware technology solutions. His firm had developed a customer relationship management (CRM) system in-house that was working very well for them.

When the market turned down in 2008 he uncovered a need among several of the firm's most important clients in the area of customer management, not his core business. Nonetheless, he saw the wisdom of helping key clients succeed in a tough market, made the appropriate arrangements to sell the in-house proprietary CRM system, and provided the support his clients needed to take advantage. The system was installed to a great reception and he soon had a revenue stream from consulting and providing support for his customers' CRM systems. Further, he was able to integrate data from many of these customers into his in-house CRM system and exploit data mining to an even greater degree. His innovation was a win for both his company and its customers.

Then these same customers asked if they could provide the CRM to their customers. Without hesitation he said yes. As a result synergies began to grow exponentially. Three levels of CRM data were now integrated and mined. Plus there was a booming business in sales, installation, consulting, and support. Altogether the CRM provided over a billion dollars in measurable, profitable revenue.

His company's policies provided a flexible foundation that allowed him to respond quickly, and to pursue and realize this opportunity even though it was outside his core business. As a result he was able to generate an unanticipated inflection point among a key group of clients and their customers. The inflection point shifted his place in the market from being simply a hardware technology provider to a business partner. This was a critical differentiator during the economic hardship of the 2008 downturn. He not only sold and installed hardware, but also worked side-by-side with his customers growing their businesses and their customers' businesses in a very challenging market.

Good foundations make possible this kind of entrepreneurial pursuit by making it possible to work with changes the market generates and use them to advantage. The lesson? Build the capacity to be flexible enough to respond to emerging opportunity.

JEANNE TISINGER OF THE CENTRAL INTELLIGENCE AGENCY ON BUILDING CAPACITY

Over the past two decades the Central Intelligence Agency's (CIA) historical mission has undergone a seismic shift as a result of the United States' changing threat landscape. To maintain operations against high-stake threats has required unprecedented information sharing and partnerships within the intelligence community. Mission requirements have increased exponentially along with data volume, variety, and velocity. Jeanne Tisinger, having been with the agency since 1983 and Chief Information Officer since 2010, has seen these changes first hand and has had a pivotal leadership role.

On the organizational front, flatter organizational structures are the norm, and people are thriving in environments where you are expected to work across teams. People can now tap into talent wherever it resides, not just in their work unit. "Big Things" are rarely done by a single person or a single box on an organizational chart.

My talent is not with spotting the specific breakthroughs. Rather, it resides in my ability to pull teams together to create what I call "coalitions of the willing" to advance our capabilities in a

Expert Input

certain area. I am surrounded by really smart people, and I love that. The workforce gets the credit for the specific innovations, and my role is to set the conditions. I try to instill a sense of purpose that matters, a culture that values new ideas and a spirit of constructive debate. I want people every day to ask themselves "How can I make what we do better?"

What is your primary role with regard to innovation?

I am here to provide a sense of purpose and create an environment where people can contribute to that purpose. While I've learned that ideas can come from anywhere, I really try to listen to those coming from the edge of the organization. In the mainstream of an organization, culture can press on people to conform to a set of accepted ideas. That is why innovation cells, skunkworks, and even just listening to restless employees often reveals the most creative new thoughts.

What will be accomplished through the CIA's Enterprise Information Technology?

This is all about knowing what our agency knows and acquiring what we seek to know. We focus on responsibly sharing it within the intelligence community wherever and whenever it will make the greatest positive impact.

Our efforts in IT are focused in what I call our four "Big Bets":

1. Revolutionize Big Data hosting, exploitation, and management
2. Accelerate operational excellence through innovation
3. Serve the CIA by supporting the Intelligence Community
4. Drive performance through talent management

By revolutionizing Big Data I mean that we will create a dynamic, massively scalable, all-source data integration and correlation environment. This will allow us to deploy and optimize huge quantities of data at previously unrealized speed. As important, the whole corpus will be continuously updated in real time.

When I talk of accelerating operational excellence I mean that we will drive best practices and innovation across the enterprise.

Serving the Intelligence Community means that CIA will innovate with the Intelligence Community space in mind, and earn a reputation for delivering and supporting best value solutions.

Driving performance through talent management highlights our continued commitment to acquiring top talent and developing that talent throughout their career. Choosing the right people, developing the right skills, to do the right work is at the heart of our workforce strategy.

As a CIO, Jeanne Tisinger was faced with mission requirements demanding much more sophisticated IT and collaboration both inside and outside her agency. She built capacity by creating coalitions of talent aligned with her well-articulated four Big Bets. Talent is a critical component of the innovation foundation that builds organizational capacity.

The Innovation Foundation

Now that we have seen the three primary pressures an innovation foundation must have the capacity to handle, I will show you how to put in place the right kind of underpinnings to transfer the stress of these inevitable forces to a strong base. This will build capacity that puts the odds of being successful in your favor. There are three elements that make up a solid innovation foundation (mentioned at the beginning of the chapter and illustrated in Figure 2.2).

Innovation relies deeply on human infrastructure to contain and successfully channel the three forces that jeopardize innovation so they support your efforts instead of tearing them down. Leadership sets the pace, overseeing all aspects of the enterprise, and continually reinforces the need for operations and innovation to coexist, managing the tension creatively. Talent brings experience and expertise to bear on market responsiveness and midwifing of new offerings. And a robust process for the emergence, development, and maturing of ideas ensures that people are continuously thinking together about how to stay ahead.

FIGURE 2.2 The Three Elements of an Innovation Foundation

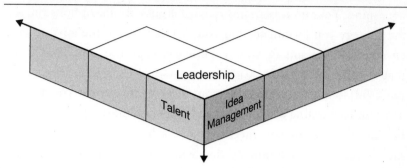

All three are expandable—as you increase each the foundation grows proportionately stronger.

"But," you may say, "innovation often happens in dysfunctional organizations...places that are clearly lacking in one if not more of these three!" Yes, it is true. In fact, every organization has its counter-productive dynamics and can be characterized as dysfunctional one way or another. And yet innovation still takes place.

If you look closely at the efforts that succeed, you will find them operating within the protection of these three elements in a microclimate. Where the microclimate stops, so does effective innovation.

If your goal is to lead an organization where innovation is a way of life, where new ideas are regularly born that reach the light of day and go on to improve your customers well-being while enhancing yours, then these three elements deserve your continuous attention and focus. Let's take a closer look at each so we can see what makes them so powerful.

Leadership

When it comes to getting innovation right, leaders must

- Talk to the right people
- Articulate the way forward
- Build partnerships

I now explain these three recommendations in more detail.

Talk to the Right People: Put simply, your most important asset is your mind. Your understanding of what is possible, the options you see, the strategy you formulate, and your assessments of the environment all come as a result of your experience, expertise, and know-how; that is, your knowledge. Aside from personal experience, your most powerful source of knowledge comes from the people you talk to. Your understanding of the world and its possibilities is most impacted by the other minds you meet. Make it a habit to identify and visit the people and environments that will provide you with maximum value as measured in fresh ideas, key learnings, and new tactics and strategies.

I first read Peter Senge's book, *The Fifth Discipline: The Art and Practice of the Learning Organization*, in the mid-1990s. At the time I was working on knowledge management at the World Bank. I was on the fledgling team that would later change the World Bank forever, propelling it onto the world stage as one of the World's Most Admired Knowledge Enterprises.

I had never heard of Senge and was impressed by his approach. He was writing about organizations that had achieved or were on their way to realizing knowledge management gains—the goal we were trying to achieve. I shared the book with my boss and peers. Steve Denning, my boss, said, "Why read when we can talk to the author?" Within a couple of weeks we were sitting in Senge's office in Cambridge discussing our organization's plans in detail with him.

Our ability to quickly meet and learn from Senge greatly accelerated our success. We experienced significant gains in the year ahead and received international recognition for our program. Part of our triumph was due to our ability to find and meet the people who could make a difference and having substantive conversations with them that expanded our thinking, provided valuable insights, and uncovered solutions to problems we were facing.

FIVE WAYS TO MEET THE RIGHT PEOPLE

1. Browse books in your chosen area of pursuit. Find the classics as well as new releases. Read them to see if the author's expertise and recommendations are a fit for your needs. Plumb the book's references (text, bibliography, index, footnotes, endorsements) for others in the field. Contact the author and any others referenced who seem like a good fit.

2. Attend conferences and consider the speakers, both keynotes and breakout sessions. People need not be celebrities to have germane experience or information. Read the program cover to cover and identify candidates for addressing your most important issues. Approach them following their presentation. Tell them what you want to talk about. Offer to contact them offline to follow up and exchange business cards.

3. Search the web. When you find people who interest you, visit their website, read something they have written, or watch a video of them to determine if their ways of thinking will be of assistance to you. Send an email with an inquiry.

4. Consult a compendium that lists thought leaders. For example, *What's the Big Idea? Creating and Capitalizing on the Best New Management Thinking* includes a listing of the top 200 business gurus from the authors' point of view.[1]

5. Ask other knowledgeable people who they consider to be experts in your field or people with relevant experience you can learn from. Often your colleagues' colleagues are an excellent resource for meeting helpful guides.

In this day and age it is relatively easy to get the email address needed to reach experts. However, the best way by far is personal introduction. But failing that consider reaching out to them through their place of business, their representative, agent, or publisher. Most of them are willing to talk to others genuinely interested in what they have to say. Keep your initial request concise, to the point. Open with a one-sentence comment that reflects your knowledge and appreciation of their work. Then get straight to the point. Keep the entire missive to less than five sentences, in consideration of their time. Likewise, request a modicum of time in response. I often will ask for only 5–10 minutes to talk. If it is clear that more time is required experts are mostly happy to accommodate as long as the conversation is on point.

Articulate the Way Forward: People rely on their leaders to craft a vision of the future that makes sense and can guide their everyday decisions. Most of the leaders I have met improvise this activity and many do it badly. Here are three tips that will help you when you speak and write about what you are working hard to accomplish through innovation:

1. **Be explicit about your conclusions and how you came to them.** First, be clear about the decisions you have reached. Share them with your people in an unvarnished fashion. Make it easy for people to understand what you are trying to do. Speak in terms they can understand and relate to. Next spell out how you came to your conclusions. Most of your staff members are not aware of your relevant experience, previous circumstances you have been part of, that lead you to make the decisions you do. When you communicate, do more than share judgment. Provide insight to your reasoning.

2. **Provide people with the opportunity to ask questions.** Be tolerant of diverse points of view and different sets of experience. When your message is viewed from multiple points of view, your key point may not be obvious to others. Let them react, inquire, challenge, and extract the information they need to satisfy their understanding. Then you will be in the best position to move forward together.

3. **Customize your message to your audience.** Make your presentation useful to their day-to-day application. Utility helps information to stick. When people realize how your message affects how they carry out their work, they will grasp it more effectively.

Communication is the first step toward coherent action. By clearly and repeatedly taking the time to spell out what you are trying to do, you will build a base of informed actors who will help you realize the fruits of innovation.

Build Partnerships: If the 21st century is typified by high-speed connectivity, business impact is typified by partnerships: two or more agencies working together to influence a network of related customers. Leadership today is largely about identifying the partnerships that will lead to broad, powerful impact and growth.

Let me be clear—I'm talking about supportive and symbiotic relationships here, not contractual business partnerships. There is a tremendous amount that can be done on the basis of mutual interest alone.

Contractual partnerships are animals unto themselves and require significant guidance beyond the scope of this book. They can be extremely valuable as well. If you are exploring contractual relationships, you must learn the plusses and minuses, the advantages and disadvantages inherent in the many varieties they come in. But for the sake of this book, I am referring to the informal variety of partnership in which mutual interest is pursued on that basis alone. Here is an example.

In the first chapter I introduced you to CEO Tony Cancelosi, who turned the Columbia Lighthouse for the Blind around. Tony is a partnership builder par excellence. In order to succeed with his veterans' program, Bridge to Work, Tony engaged multiple partners. Not only does he participate in four local government workforce development councils, but he also attends and creates events that are designed to bring movers and shakers together.

One of his primary tools is an advisory board that is an ongoing assembly of some of the best minds in Washington, DC. He has brought together investors, academicians, respected journalists, social activists, military generals, strategy experts, marketing authorities, business leaders, and local celebrities. While not formal business partnerships, these valuable relationships provide strategic allies and a sounding board (consisting of those "right people" I advise you to talk to).

Every quarter this group assembles to learn what Tony has been up to and lend their support to the strategy he has put in place for the Lighthouse. At each session new people are introduced and have the opportunity to network. Tony is the ringleader, and the advisory board delivers, creating results on a volunteer basis. In 2011 the Lighthouse did its first Light the Way 5k run. Thanks to the efforts of the advisory board over $80,000 in profit was raised. Since these allies were not contractual partners, there was no financial relationship requiring splitting those proceeds among the partners. CLB realized every penny for underwriting its charitable activities.

In 2012, only its second year, the 5k was co-chaired by Mark Lerner, principal owner of the Washington Nationals, and Steve Neibergall, president of the Eastern Division of Safeway. These powerful sponsors came in the door through Tony's ability to forge partnerships.

Here are three tips to building informal partnerships that will help you get innovation right:

1. **Be clear about what you hope to get out of the partnership.** Take the time to define why the partnership is important to you and your partner. Get to the value that makes it worth pursuing.

2. **Share the goals of the partnership with others who have a stake in its success.** Do this through informal conversations, over the phone, via email, over coffee. Individuals to consider include

   - Clients
   - Prospects
   - Customers
   - Vendors
   - Industry experts
   - People who work for regulatory groups
   - Communities
   - Investors
   - People in the trade media and business press

- Executives and employees of similar organizations

These conversations will educate you, providing you with multiple perspectives on how to get the most out of your partnership. Share what you learn with your partners.

3. **Take accountability for coordination of partnership activities.** This includes identifying important issues as they arise. Be the one who identifies and handles the critical issues. Take responsibility for planning and facilitating joint events. Enable all critical interactions to go as smoothly as possible. Foster joint development for every party involved.

- Coordinate product and service development, including joint documents and websites. Make it your business to succeed by doing the necessary groundwork so everyone is happy with the results.

- Provide regular assessment of the partnership; take a proactive stance to keep things on the right track. Consider developing a scorecard with input from each partner. Use it as a way to review progress and identify issues before they become problems.

The three primary sources required of innovative leaders — talking to the right people, articulating the way forward, and building partnerships — work together. Together they ensure your leadership is well informed, a source of unambiguous guidance, and reinforced by powerful allies. This places leadership in strong, healthy condition as one of the three mutually reinforcing faces of your innovation foundation.

Talent

Second only to you in impact are the people who work for you. The more influence they have, the more important their talent is. To scale your ability to acquire and develop talent, you need a chief human resources officer (CHRO) who understands your goals. The CHRO is in a unique position to drive innovation capacity when he or she is fully aligned with business goals. The CHRO has the capacity to proactively recruit, bring in tomorrow's leaders, and identify candidates who will fulfill innovation objectives. Securing people who understand and embrace the power of innovation is of the utmost importance. You need to hire people with specific qualities. They must be

1. **Unafraid of challenge.** Bring in people who are turned on by the challenges you are facing and opportunities to be harvested.
2. **Success driven.** Find people who look failure in the eye and see it as the feedback they need to achieve their goals without losing energy.
3. **Proactive about intelligence.** Seek professionals who know how to find the information and knowledge you need to achieve measurable impact in the areas critical to your innovation initiatives.
4. **Experts at interdependence.** Locate talent that knows how to work professional relationships and team communication, yet does not shy away from developing their own expertise and driving force.

And finally they must possess

5. **Strategic and tactical skills.** Pull in high performers who excel at thinking at a high level, as well as capturing the next important win.

When you have acquired or developed key leaders with these specific qualities, you have built core capacity for innovation. To continue to expand and grow this capability, provide ongoing professional development in each of these five areas.

To give you a clear idea of what is possible when you join forces with your CHRO, let's take a look at Holly Kortright, CHRO at Deltek, Inc. The company has undergone radical growth over the last several years, including domestic and international acquisitions. Holly has played a key role in Deltek's growth with her love for designing systems and managing change.

She is passionate about working with her CEO, executives, and other members of internal leadership teams to help them create the change that propels the business forward. She has worked on a variety of large-scale human capital strategy projects, coached teams of employees in how to change the way they operate, and aligned her HR team with the strategic objectives of the company.

Says her boss, CEO Kevin Parker, "One of the things I appreciate about Holly is that she sees herself as a member of the senior strategic team and aligns everything she does with our business objectives. She is the guardian of Deltek's culture and the direction of the organization. She is not an HR leader who thinks like a business person, she is a business leader with a specialty in HR."[2]

As with Deltek, you need a CHRO like Kortright who will bring in new talent and develop your current people so they generate the future you want.

Idea Management

The third face of the cornerstone for a strong innovation foundation is *idea management*. Finding and developing the right ideas is a key business challenge of innovation. Rarely are businesses short on ideas — it is *good* ideas that are in short supply. And what makes a good idea? They almost never appear fully formed. Instead they arise immature and in need of help to grow into something that will have strategic impact.

Here are some of the challenges idea management addresses:

- How do we capture, prioritize, and organize our ideas?
- Which do we hold on to and which do we toss aside?
- How do we develop the ideas we keep to support our business objectives?
- How do we engage critical stakeholders in the process?
- How do we make it easy enough for everyone to participate, yet robust enough to develop real business solutions?
- How do we sidestep political correctness and work around biases?
- How do we go from intangible discussion to practical solutions?
- How do we operationalize our ideas?

There are three requirements to answering these questions productively:

1. *A leadership mandate*: A clear articulation by leadership on the innovation priorities of the organization.
2. *Easy access*: An effortless way for stakeholders to contribute and participate

3. *Robust development*: Processes that allow people to work together to winnow and grow the most valuable ideas.

Let's consider each more closely.

Leadership Mandate: It is leadership's responsibility to direct the actions of the organization to ensure all activity is aligned with strategic priorities. That is why the initial message must come from the center of command. In general there should be no more than three high-level strategic priorities. More than that and just tracking the follow-up activities will diffuse progress significantly.

Examples of leadership messages:

- We will lead the way on cutting medical costs by 15% while improving care.
- We will be first to market in defense with water-propelled torpedoes.
- Our schools will become a center of excellence and a national example.

What makes these messages good is that they are concise, unambiguous, and stated in terms of measurable outcomes. Each is no more than a single, short sentence. They are to the point and do not mince words. They draw a line in the sand. Rather than using vague, difficult-to-define words they make bold statements that are easy to measure: "cut costs by 15%," "first to market," and "national example."

Ill-formed leadership messages do more harm than good. They create disagreements rather than unification among the ranks. They have the opposite qualities of those just mentioned. They are rambling, lengthy, vague, and devoid of measurable outcomes.

Easy Access: Effective idea management relies on people from all corners to pool their thoughts and work together to build robust solutions. There needs to be an uncomplicated, even fun, entry process that encourages everyone to participate. It should be easy to access.

An excellent model for this can be found among popular children's websites that rely on their ease of initial use and fun interface to attract participation. These sites are visually stimulating, not overly cluttered; they use images meaningful to their audience that have positive associations and include a variety of easy-to-use entry points that lead to encouraging experiences.

To apply this to a business environment, you would of course have to transpose both the age and the content appropriateness to the work at hand. But the principles can be applied directly: inspire, provide stimulating and clear messaging, make it easy for the user to get results they appreciate, stay on theme using all elements to reinforce the primary purpose.

Robust Development: Idea development is both art and science. The best methods for managing ideas have a disciplined process that allows for people to have a good time, try out a lot of half-baked notions in the company of interested experts, and work together to mature an idea.

The three critical tasks of a strong idea development protocol are

1. Maturation
2. Evaluation
3. Trials

Let's consider each in more detail.

Maturation   When ideas first become visible most are in a nascent stage. This is true even of an idea that has been developed over years of thinking if it has not been allowed to grow and develop in the presence of knowledgeable colleagues.

For ideas to mature to the point where their kernel or essence becomes clear takes some handling by diverse parties. Business is a complex arena and something that appears to fly in one area may not make it off the ground in another.

One of my clients wanted to increase subscription for her organization's journal and came up with the idea of offering a substantial cash prize to anyone who could increase the subscriber base by 50% in a given year. She developed the idea on her own for a year, shared it with several key members of her board, and even moved it through board approval.

Meanwhile her senior staff team was abuzz with concern. A lot of the details had not been worked out. It wasn't clear what the guidelines for the subscriptions were. There were no business processes in place to track the kind of highly unusual activity such a large cash prize was sure to generate. From each person's point of view, something critical was missing. Until they had a chance to resolve the issues, the idea was immature, not ready for prime time.

Solid idea development takes place via the collaborative efforts of qualified experts. Experts include not only those who hold credentials, but also those with frontline responsibility who will be impacted by the idea in execution.

Evaluation   Once an idea has been developed to the point that it is clear what is intended, leaders must judge whether or not it warrants further resources.

An idea can be mature, easily understood, clear in its intended impact, and still be an inappropriate spend of resources. There must be an evaluation process that tosses aside those ideas that do not contribute to the organization's strategic thrust.

And so there needs to be a clear gateway through which ideas pass and are evaluated for continued funding. The decision process should be transparent so everyone who was involved in the maturation process can understand why a particular idea does or does not pass through this gate.

Having access to the criteria and seeing it in action provides feedback to the developers. A clear understanding of what caused an idea to fail at the evaluation stage will be a great help when other ideas are being developed. Going forward, they will know how to better mature ideas so they have a higher incidence of success.

Trials   After an idea has successfully passed through evaluation it still must prove itself in a test. This avoids funding innovations built on unproven ideas.

For example, it became clear at the World Bank during the initiative I described in the introduction that we needed communities to prosper and propagate. Based on frontline research of existing groups in the organization we discovered these communities worked best when their leader was both (a) a world-class expert, and (b) very good at networking and facilitation.

We had plenty of world-class experts. However, almost none of them were skilled at networking and facilitation. Our idea was to create a cadre of leaders who were both experts and savvy in social skills. These, we had reason to believe, would form and lead communities across the planet. Our first trial was to train the experts on hand.

Classes were developed. Invitations were sent out. Of the one hundred invited only five showed. After contacting the others we discovered none of them had any interest in picking up the skill set we were offering. Most saw it as a waste of time. They were primarily interested in pursuing the esoteric research that made them a world-class expert in the first place.

The first trial of our idea was a failure. But the experiment was worthy. As a result we saw another way forward. We would find another professional who was socially savvy and pair him or her with the expert. So, we thought, two people would lead most of our communities.

We asked the experts to participate in the communities we created in exchange for the support of their new colleague whose duties would include doing menial work that would free up the expert's time.

In less than a year we had over one hundred communities across the globe. Our second trial was a success.

PAUL PLUSCHKELL OF SPIGIT ON IDEA MANAGEMENT

Paul Pluschkell founded Spigit in 2007 based on his experience working in finance with content, information technology, and algorithmic trading. Spigit provides software that helps organizations capture, rank, and execute the best ideas from employees, customers, and partners. They use crowdsourcing (outsourcing tasks to a distributed

Expert Input

Expert Input

group of people), game mechanics (rules intended to produce enjoy-able play), and big data analytics (tools for working with data sets too large and complex to analyze with traditional database manage-ment tools) to come up with the best ideas for growing revenue and reducing costs while expanding employee and customer engagement. Among Spigits 1,000+ clients are Coca Cola, Overstock.com, Estee Lauder, Southwest Airlines, SAP, Cisco, JC Penney, New York City, and Hartford County. ·

Pluschkell's story illustrates my approach to idea management, supported by a leadership mandate, easy access, and robust develop-ment. One of his game-changing insights—achieved while watching his daughter play—is that game mechanics stimulate engagement at any age. From engagement, innovation flows.

When we entered the market, an executive's idea of innovation was putting a few of their brightest people in the room and seeing what they could do. It is now a necessity to figure out how to empower all their employees to contribute no matter where and when they work. Because everyone is connected, we are for the first time in a position where each person can be engaged in relevant topics aligned with business strategies and pitted against real outcomes.

My background is in the financial markets. Where I worked we would take information right off the exchange, run it to a bank of computers where our analysts could immediately apply advanced analytics. There was no lag between getting the information and analyzing it, and this created tremendous advantage.

We can now do the same thing with ideas in organizations. This includes, for example, systematically ridding an enterprise of inefficiencies, identifying the next billion-dollar idea, or taking existing offerings and ratcheting them up to an unheard-of level of performance.

How do you get productive engagement?

When we were first building the software I was watching my daughter playing with Webkinz. She would buy these little stuffed animals and get access to their website for six months. I watched her get currency and buy things for her animal, building it a bigger house and putting in a swimming pool. I made all our developers get a second screen and put Webkinz on it so they could play. From Day 1 we were putting in game mechanics. I wanted the developers to create the intense engagement young children feel when their stuffed animals come to life and they can play with them.

We look at engagement as a recipe of three things:

1. Participation
2. Collaboration
3. Innovation

We correlate these three and it comes out to an engagement score. The engagement score is the key to our community. We drive that through social behavior and mechanics literally drawn from video games to make sure we are attracting the right crowd to the right problem at the right time. From play comes engagement, and from engagement innovation flows.

What is it that makes crowd-sourced idea management software work so well?

People are broader than their job titles. They want to be helpful. If you give them transparency into what your company's challenges are, they are prone to both increasing productivity and helping you at a cause even when it is outside their domain.

Using that as the fuel for participation, you also need a road map, a clear way to participate, and tools that help you succeed. Getting a solid understanding of what it takes to do innovation right and being helped along the way is invaluable. The tools Spigit provides takes everything to another level.

You must be connected to the key initiatives of the organization. Idea management software forces your hand on this, as you must define just one or a very small number of initiatives to work on. This is the scope that ensures that every conversation, every team, every breakout is pushing your organization in the direction it needs to go. Then, the power of the crowd kicks in and the results are profound.

As founder of the premier idea management system, Spigit, Paul Pluschkell worked hard to make his software easy to use, robust, and practical. He did that by drawing on the same principles used to make children's games fun, enrolling participants in the collaborative development of ideas that contribute directly to an organization's strategic goals. This approach works well to get people involved and engaged.

The collective maturation and refinement that takes place as people work together on pertinent ideas ripens them for selection and execution. Idea management that accomplishes these difficult tasks makes a real contribution to an organization's innovation capacity.

A Sturdy Foundation Supports Success

Leadership, talent management, and idea management work together in a powerful trio. Done well they create a solid innovation foundation. When the inevitable stresses of operational pressures, innovation itself, and a shifting market exert their power, it is these three in combination that form the base that is able to use that stress to make your organization stronger.

This is what happens when the right people with the right attitude systematically identify new ideas and mature and winnow them before decisively bringing them to test. This is what provides a healthy relationship between operations and innovation. With this foundation in place your organization will have the capacity to reliably respond to unanticipated challenges and opportunities. You will experience a level of support that will not only survive storms but also allow you to do your best work.

Success Rules

- Three forces can bring down a company: operational pressures, innovation stress, and changing market forces.

- The three interdependent components of an innovation foundation include leadership, talent management, and idea management.
- Leaders create a solid underpinning for innovation through talking to the right people, articulating the way forward, and building partnerships.
- Hire and develop people who understand and embrace the power of innovation.
- Finding and developing the right ideas is a key business challenge of innovation, requiring a leadership mandate, stakeholder contribution, and robust development of winning ideas.

Collect Intelligence

Intelligence is information that supports your ability to make strategic decisions. It could be information about products, customers, competitors, the market or internal capabilities—or all of the above. Effective innovation requires intelligence to make smart choices that take into account each of these areas.

I have been collecting intelligence for my executive clients since 2000. I find it surprising that so many have little or no intelligence efforts in-house, let alone the ability to exploit this resource. It's a stark absence. They cannot act on their information because they have none or what they have is haphazard, built upon conversation and hunches only. It is a sad state considering that much of this valuable input is readily available for a negligible cost.

Intelligence done right provides valuable, legal data germane to any innovation effort. The *Wall Street Journal* (WSJ) is an example of an intelligence tool for the business masses. It provides leaders with an edge in the marketplace. It does this by furnishing critical, publicly available news and information in a format that makes it easy to find relevant content. If you read the WSJ you are several steps ahead of competitors who do not. To enable effective innovation you need your own private WSJ, customized to your organization, your clients, and your value-drivers.

Intelligence improves innovation by checking your hunches, identifying weaknesses, targeting opportunities, providing market insight, and drawing valuable input from your customers. It is beneficial before, during, and after innovation takes place.

Good intelligence is the basis for identifying opportunities for innovation. It is perhaps the single most powerful way to systematically uncover new profitable revenue streams and more efficient ways to serve your customers. It also makes undue risk visible for what may otherwise appear to be a good idea.

During an innovation initiative, robust intelligence can refine the quality of your work, keep you pointed in the right direction, and affirm or deny the value of the innovation in the marketplace. By directing the intelligence effort to address performance improvement while you are in execution you can even increase the amount of impact your innovation will have.

After you have launched an initiative, gathering intelligence is a valuable way to stay in touch with the realities of execution. Done smartly it can tighten your relationship to on-the-ground implementation, bringing you closer to customers and other critical stakeholders.

The Three Areas of Focus for Intelligence

Typical intelligence efforts explore three interrelated areas.

1. Customers
2. Market conditions
3. Organizational capabilities

By combining information from all three, you assemble an explanation of how an organization is doing along with potential challenges and opportunities, and you get a good idea of what needs to be done so the organization can handle the challenges well and take advantage of the opportunities.

Customers

The fundamental questions to answer are, *Who are our customers?* and *How are we doing at serving them?* That is, who are we serving and how well are we meeting their needs?

For most organizations these are more complex questions to answer than it would first appear. For example, it is normal to learn that you have several important sets of customers and among them some are happy, others are not, and some feel neutral. It is also normal to learn that you are meeting some needs, missing some, and could be doing better concerning others.

For example, I work with Doug Culkin, CEO of the National Apartment Association (NAA). His company is the leading advocate for quality rental housing in the United States. NAA's member companies provide housing for over 100 million Americans and include owners, managers, developers, and suppliers.

One of the services his customers value most is the education he provides, which measurably improves the performance of the frontline staff who operate rental properties by providing them with the tools and knowledge they need to achieve and maintain high levels of professionalism and performance improvement in their work.

The rental industry is on a growth curve, as is Doug's organization. In the 13 years since Doug took the helm in 1999 the organization has grown from a mom-and-pop operation that was facing real budget challenges to a robust $23 million-and-growing association.

He hired me to collect the intelligence he needs to grow aggressively. Growth was slowing and he wanted to accelerate again. With a better understanding of the market, his customers, and his organization's capabilities, he would make the necessary changes to quicken growth.

I conducted my standard process, following the steps I describe later in this chapter. My efforts revealed that his association was doing well serving the rental property owners by educating frontline staff and improving their performance. But there was a good deal more that could be done to serve market leaders, including large scale investors.

This group would provide the NAA with greater influence in their current advocacy work and enable three new benefits—access to the top echelon that would complement their existing strength at the grass roots, knowledge that would benefit the entire industry, and overall increased capability to serve the industry.

Because NAA has a reputation for educational excellence and a number of solid relationships with investors, Culkin was in a position to identify key offerings that would be of value to market leaders and try them out. This will require significant work. The vast majority of NAA's current marketing efforts, services, and content were geared toward rental unit operators, a decidedly different crowd.

Nonetheless, as a leader himself Culkin understood the choice and decided to pursue the opportunity to take advantage of the inflection point that would come from bringing this powerful community into his organization.

As a result of our work together he kicked off a new initiative, owned at the top by himself and his senior management team, to build relationships with key investors, learn how the NAA can provide unequivocal value, and begin trial offerings to learn what captures the interest of other industry leaders.

Thus, an intelligence focus on customers revealed an emerging category for the NAA with significant potential.

Market Conditions

Market conditions have many variables and are in constant flux. As a result they are much more complex to track than customers. However, market conditions play a role in the success of every organization.

Using the NAA example I will illustrate the identification of important market conditions.

Three large market factors are influencing the rental industry. First, the mortgage crisis of 2008. Second, America's 2008–2009 economic downturn and the corresponding slow recovery. The third is urbanization.

As a result of the end of the 2006 housing boom and the ensuing mortgage crisis, approximately 4 million families have gone through foreclosure in the United States between 2007–2012,[1] leaving them without a home they own and forcing them into a variety of living conditions including many who now rent.

Due to the slow recovery from the 2008–2009 recession, more Americans are choosing to rent.[2] The US Census shows rental vacancies in first quarter 2012[3] to be the lowest in ten years.[4] This is caused by a variety of factors, including unemployment, which makes it difficult for people to either afford or qualify for a mortgage; homes being taken off the market; home prices under continued pressure, thus keeping homes from going on the market; and another rise in foreclosure activity. As a result of these factors rentals are up.

Urban areas continue to grow with already 82% of the US population living in them and a national average rate of urbanization at 1.2%.[5] Growth of the inner city is closely linked to rental increases due to the limited number of houses available.

All of these conditions influence the state of the rental industry and are important to include in any business intelligence effort. Similarly, market conditions that impact your sector and business must be identified to provide important information for strategic decision making—including decisions associated with innovation.

Organizational Capabilities

A good, strong business intelligence effort evaluates your ability to act and seize opportunity through innovation. This requires assessing your ability to design and deliver value to your customers in the current market. To do this, the intelligence must make clear your deficiencies as well as your assets.

Areas to assess include

- Talent—Do you have the professionals in the pipeline to deliver on innovations when they hit the market? Is training required to do well in the short-term future? A good intelligence effort explores whether you have the talent needed to understand, design, and execute innovation opportunities while facing expected challenges.
- Resources — Will you have enough time, people, and money at the right moment to undergird the resources required for innovation? This includes especially the first dip before your offering goes live, when costs are up and you have not yet had the chance to generate revenue. (For more on this, see the "Innovation Profit

Cycle" in Chapter 6.) Innovation has clear needs, and resources must be apportioned to support your efforts.

- Ability to respond — As circumstances shift and change, are you positioned well to take advantage? The ability to be responsive is critical to ensure that you are both able to take advantage of fortune and to correct course as new offerings roll out, thus making the best of circumstances and ramping up to production as quickly as possible.

- Systems — Do you have the right information technology, and is it optimized for innovation? Your systems must support the business processes that make innovation a success, from internal tracking and monitoring to every point that you touch the customer.

- Data — Are you collecting the right information? Are your data collection systems robust? Do you have the ability to correlate important pieces of information, and are the right people reviewing the results? Data is one of the most powerful tools every organization has at its disposal. To serve your innovation efforts it must provide you with the information you need to generate value for your customers.

Let's go back to the NAA to complete my example.

In the area of *talent* they scored high on existing staff with a strong, entrepreneurial leader and capable senior team members. Three positions were missing, however — a chief marketing officer to lead a world-class marketing program, a chief information officer to take their data and systems to a new level of operation, and a dedicated researcher to provide proprietary high-quality reports and briefings to members.

Resources were in good shape with the success of their business under Culkin's leadership.

Ability to respond was dampened by the need to improve the relationship with their affiliates, the local organizations they worked with, to reach and provide critical services to members. The business intelligence yielded several options for improving these relationships, including the identification of areas to target that the affiliates would be most responsive to, and key volunteer leaders who stood ready to assist.

Systems were already being improved prior to the intelligence report.

Data was in need of an overhaul to ensure the best possible information on members, affiliates, and programs. A comprehensive data cleansing program was outlined as part of the intelligence report.

Culkin began to implement many of the recommendations immediately and took those requiring oversight and input to his executive committee and board for review. The recommendations were endorsed and execution is taking place as this book goes to press. The intelligence was written up and presented to the executive committee, providing them with documentation of the process, sources of the intelligence, and recommendations to discuss. My activity with the senior management team indicates an increase in performance is already under way.

From this example, simplified for presentation here, you get a clear idea of the intelligence NAA gathered to help them target dramatic growth over the next two to three years, all obtained from covering the three primary areas.

Intelligence concerning each of the three areas — customers, market conditions, and organizational capabilities — will help you define the areas to single out for focus in your innovation efforts.

Now that we have looked at the areas that business intelligence focuses on, it is time to get into what makes a good effort as it applies to getting innovation right.

The Eight Steps of an Intelligence Effort

Because outcomes, scope, and circumstances vary, every intelligence effort is different. However, every effort should include the following eight core steps in sequence:

1. Define scope
2. Determine goals
3. Consult data sources, news media, and trend experts

4. Conduct interviews with key stakeholders
5. Secret shopping to test quality from customers' perspective
6. Iteratively share results and receive direction
7. Due diligence for controversial, high-value, and high-risk issues
8. Format and present results for maximum impact

Let's take a closer look at each.

Step 1. Define Scope

This is the foundation of your intelligence gathering. You must get this right or your effort runs the risk of being a waste of time and attention. Scope identifies the segment of the business you are examining. It sets the focus and the limits of the effort.

For example, I provided intelligence to a trade association that was experiencing significant growth yet had penetrated only 27% of the market. They wanted to innovate in order to aggressively grow their member base, achieving a Vertical Climb inflection point. The scope of this project was *membership acquisition*.

Three questions will help you determine scope:

1. What aspect of your business do you want to improve?
2. How will this intelligence effort generate success for you?
3. In the best of all circumstances, how will your situation progress?

The answers to these questions will point you to the part of your business that is the scope of your effort. When you understand what aspect of your business you are seeking to improve, you have limited your view to only that which is helpful. By having a clear scope, you constrain yourself to the intelligence that will make the best impact on your innovation efforts.

Further, by defining scope, you also force yourself to think about how you will use the information produced and to consider whether the costs and benefits generated to gain that information are worth the investment.

Step 2. Determine Goals

You are gathering intelligence specifically to achieve business goals. This is the place to be clear about them. These are the objectives your intelligence will satisfy.

In my example with the trade association, my number one goal was to *gather the intelligence required to increase penetration in their target market*. Below that I had three subgoals. When the subgoals were satisfied, the number one goal would be achieved. We wrote it out like this:

Intelligence will help define:

- Value-drivers that will succeed in attracting those who are not yet members.
- Barriers to entry for that portion of the market that has not yet joined.
- Innovation initiatives that support the national organization and local chapters to work together to harvest a greater percentage of the market.

Your goals should be clearly stated and easily understood by every stakeholder in the intelligence effort, including the agent carrying out the effort, you, and any partners involved.

Step 3. Consult Data Sources, News Media, and Trend Experts

With the World Wide Web at your fingertips, data sources, news media, and trend experts are reachable like never before. Every business intelligence provider will have a plethora of resources to draw upon.

There are also industry-specific and client-specific resources that you, your team, and your front-line staff will be aware of. Be sure to provide these to your agent so he or she can take these additional resources into consideration while putting together a plan of action.

For example, when I began the business intelligence effort for Culkin of the National Apartment Association, he introduced me to the work of Chris Lee on trends in the real estate industry.[6]

This step is ongoing and continues right up to the end. It does not stop when Step 4 commences.

Step 4. Conduct Interviews with Key Stakeholder Groups

A good intelligence effort will include candid conversations with the people who matter. Your stakeholders are your most important resource. Their concerns and desires are the source of your success when it comes to innovation.

This is one reason you must have a neutral outsider conduct the work for you. It is critical that you are able to get untainted responses that portray sentiments with accuracy and without pulling punches. To the degree that you achieve candor, you will have a solid foundation on which to build your understanding of market feelings, thoughts, attitudes, opinions, and beliefs. You will be able to *tell it like it is*.

There are many varieties of stakeholders and most are germane to innovation. Beyond the obvious group—your customers—there are a wide variety of partners in a number of roles who will have to participate cooperatively for your innovation to be a success.

For my clients I have developed the following list of 14 categories of stakeholders. I use this list to help them identify those we should interview.

1. Political leaders

    Will your innovations rely on the support of politicians either elected or running for election? If so, they must be included.

2. Policymakers

    If any kind of law or protocol must be introduced or crafted to support the success of your new products or services, spend time understanding your policymakers' points of view.

3. Resource providers

    It is not unusual for new programs to require a change in resource allocation. Whether it is shifting people, money, or activity, be sure to include the decision makers who will determine how resources are positioned.

4. Influencers

The success of a new offering often relies on people who shape the opinions of your customers. Interviewing them will help you to see the world the way they do and understand the concerns that will drive their behavior in response to your innovations.

5. Thought leaders

It behooves you to understand how your innovation fits in with other future trends and the benefits it will be positioned to generate. Thought leaders in your field can help you think this through.

6. Technical experts

More risk and opportunity rides on the insights of technical experts than we like to imagine. Be sure to consult with those whose area of expertise overlaps with your new offerings.

7. Researchers and academicians

Academia and other bastions of research often want to understand the impact of innovations. Their attention sometimes confers credibility. Investigate to see if your intelligence would benefit from their perspectives and concerns.

8. Practical visionaries

Out on the bleeding edge you will sometimes find people who have experience that you can use to benefit your projects — including experience that will allow you to avoid mistakes they have made.

9. Frontline executers

Always include the people who have experience at the front lines. They know the customers like no one else and have insights that come from first-hand experience.

10. Partners

If you will depend on others to make your innovations a success, be sure to include them as you gather intelligence.

11. **Alliances**

    When you are acting in alliance with others (not always the case), they become a critical source.

12. **Suppliers**

    Suppliers are important for two reasons: often their business will be directly impacted by innovations, and they are sensitive to pressures and conditions that can have an impact on your success.

13. **Competitors**

    This is undoubtedly a difficult group to interview because they have a vested interest in your failure. Nonetheless, no other party understands your predicament as intimately as the competition. If you have a way of understanding their point of view, it can be immensely helpful.

14. **Detractors**

    These are the people, other than competitors, who would prefer to see you go out of business. This perspective can be important, albeit uncomfortable. To their dismay they can furnish you with some of the most important intelligence you will come across. If you listen carefully, they will show you your weak spots and you can bolster those in response. This will give you a greater advantage when you go to market.

Interviews are a source of great information, much of it irreplaceable. Go through the list above and determine which of these 14 you must add to your interview list.

Step 5. Secret Shopping

While there are many methods for getting inside the skin of your customers, secret shopping refers to engaging in an undercover customer experience. It is one of the best ways to understand what your patrons go through. To do this, your intelligence agent simply engages your workforce as a typical customer without revealing his or her true identity. By personally experiencing what your customers go through as they attempt to procure and use your products and services, he or she will gain invaluable insight into your business. Request that the person gathering intelligence engages more than once so that anomalies are easily spotted.

You will be amazed at the results from this one exercise. The information you can gain through this very simple act is generally nothing short of extraordinary. Whether or not these results are a surprise to you, having these experiences included in your intelligence report will force you to decide how or if you want to act on what you know.

There are many aspects of the customer experience that are important to fully understand. Figure 3.1 presents the ten stages of the customer's journey I use in my work when conducting business intelligence.

Each of these stages represents an opportunity for the relationship to propel you in the market or thwart your progress. Your innovations will have to move through all ten of these stages to be truly successful.

I first became aware of the ten stages as a customer. I realized that most businesses tended to provide quality customer care only when there was a transaction at stake. Their post-transactional care varied widely, with the great majority being less than satisfying.

I decided to map all the intersections I had with a particular service with attention to the opportunities that the provider had to strengthen their bond with me. Since doing so I have been able to use this technique very successfully with a number of organizations to increase the number of opportunities for developing productive relationships with customers.

Handled well, each stage results in greater engagement and a deeper commitment to going forward together. Handled poorly, each is an opportunity for the customer to bail on the relationship and go elsewhere, or even foment bad relations. That is why the ten stages are important to study in an intelligence effort, and secret shopping is an excellent way to do it.

Step 6. Iteratively Share Results and Receive Direction

Because intelligence gathering serves your decision making, it is critical that the agent comes back to you regularly, shares the ongoing results

FIGURE 3.1 The Ten Stages of the Customer Journey

1. First Exposure

This occurs through media (Internet, radio, TV, posters, direct mail) and word-of-mouth. The opportunity here is to consider how news of your innovation reaches your customers even before they meet you.

2. First Contact

This is the initial touch point with your client, the first time the client engages you directly. It could be a call to inquire or a preliminary visit to your website. This is when first impressions are made. You have a unique window to win your client's approval that won't be repeated.

3. First Engagement

The first time a client requests something of you is the first chance you have to build a relationship. If things go wrong, it is the time to jump in and right them. If things go well, you are off to a good start.

4. Deepening of the Relationship

This happens one of two ways: the customer is seriously considering a purchase, or something goes awry in the fledgling relationship. Either way it is a special happening that carries with it the possibility of bonding. It all depends on how it is handled.

5. First Sale

Now the client has made the choice to do business with you. This is a high-potential interaction with the power to forge synergy for the future or devolve into a regret. For the first time you are truly in a position to either succeed or fail.

6. First Question or Need

In this situation the customer is reaching out with an unmet need. It is generally a decision point in the relationship, formed around your response. This is an opportunity to show you have the customer's best interest in mind.

7. Brand Development

Your brand develops through the ongoing experience your customers have of your product or service. They are either satisfied or not, and that will form their image of you and of your ability to deliver on their needs.

FIGURE 3.1 continued

8. Reinforcing Business

In this stage your customers are taking actions that reinforce their relationship with you. This could be through buying complementary offerings or building upon their purchases, cementing them into their way of life. This is a risk for the clients as they are making themselves more dependent on you. If you come through, you may be able to count them as your advocates. Otherwise you risk not only losing their business but also turning them into a voice against you.

9. Repeat Business

Here clients make a choice about their ongoing relationship with you. Either they come to you when they are in need again or they go somewhere else. The opportunity here is to win their allegiance as an ongoing customer. The danger is that you can lose their loyalty as they walk away.

10. Client as evangelist

Now you have clients with a real investment in the relationship. So much so that they will speak out about the customer experience, good or bad. If you have been severely disappointing they can hit their social media with just as much vehemence as if you are a favorite. Do you make it easy for them to speak out? Are you there when they decry your offerings, ready to respond and right the situation?

of the intelligence gathering, and receives redirection in order to achieve the best possible results.

It is like checking a compass as you journey toward a destination off the map. The agent's regular return to leadership to share findings and get continued guidance makes it possible for the organization to end up at the desired location, helping you achieve objectives and make the best possible decisions for business success.

In 2006 I was working with the director of the Peace Corps, Gaddi Vasquez. We were focused on designing inflection points that would help the Peace Corps deal with three trends requiring a strategic response: the introduction of technology to the volunteer experience, the changing demographics of America, and building IT infrastructure for the organization to take it into the 21st century.

After conducting several focus groups and conferring with members of his senior management team I brought the recommendations back to him for consideration. The way forward seemed arduous but necessary. In the middle of our session together Gaddi had a eureka moment and diagramed a new way forward that was practical, efficient, and powerful. If I had not called that meeting to share my results and receive his direction our work together would have taken an entirely different route that would not have benefited from his insight.

Checking back in regularly with leadership is a must. It pulls together the best of both worlds: intelligence results and leadership guidance.

Step 7. Due Diligence for Controversial, High-Value, and High-Risk Issues

You may know in advance that you are considering innovation in an especially risky environment, striking out without full support from your primary stakeholders—perhaps proceeding amidst vociferous objections from key players—or have your eye on a lucrative opportunity that could completely change your game if you are victorious. Or you may discover along the way that the road to success is paved with land mines, key stakeholders are preparing to bolt, or the cost of missing the target is extremely high.

In these situations due diligence is required to ensure that you investigate and unearth all relevant information that will contribute to your success or prevent you from making a costly mistake.

Controversial circumstances include pursuing an innovation that will forever change your relationship with some of your most valuable players. These may be customers but they might also be vendors, suppliers, advocates, policymakers, industry thought leaders, partners, alliance members, internal leaders, or competitors.

If you set out on a path that fundamentally shifts your location in the market's ecosystem, you must prepare by learning as much as you can and doing your very best to anticipate the results. Shifts in an ecosystem can have surprising results.

Four Tactics for Getting Due Diligence Right: High risk *demands* intelligence. You must pursue information that will inform you about the details of the risk and help you formulate possible outcomes if you pursue this particular course of action, their likelihood of occurring, and strategies for coping in different circumstances.

High returns also demand care. If you are going for the gold and there is significant treasure at stake, you want to get it right the first time or as close to right as you can manage. You must be well prepared before you act and ready when the time to strike comes. Intelligence can provide the background you need to ensure you are at your best and all systems are in place to handle implementation.

Here are four due diligence tactics that you can use when faced with high-risk situations:

1. **Pull together a S.W.A.T Team (Special Weapons and Tactics).** These are veterans with specialized tools (weapons) and skill sets (tactics) who can go into a high-stakes situation and execute well under pressure. Their experience provides them with the knowledge required to make the right decisions in a high-risk environment and their expertise allows you to rely on their results. Here are five guidelines for creating and using your S.W.A.T. team.

a. Identify trusted professionals you can rely upon. Choose them using three criteria. They must be able to (1) process confidential information, (2) apply relevant skill and experience, and (3) work constructively within your intelligence effort.

b. Assemble your team and explain why you chose them, the circumstances of your concern, and the uniqueness of their mission.

c. Set specific, clearly articulated goals. For example, *Determine if the market will favor acquisition of our chief competitor. Produce a report to document findings, reasoning, and recommendations.*

d. Convene them in parallel to the larger intelligence initiative. Have them focus only on the area that is of great concern. A S.W.A.T. Team should be dedicated only to the high-risk task, not used for general intelligence work.

e. When their task is done, disband the team. Their efforts should be intensive, time-bound, and cease when their mission is accomplished.

2. **Identify legal parameters.** A tenet of all intelligence gathering is that you never break the law. When risk is high you want to ensure that your actions are appropriate. Bring in your counsel to review what you are doing and ask them to clarify any extra precautions that are required.

3. **Educate yourself.** Although you are working with intelligence experts, seasoned veterans, and legal counsel, you must never cede your authority or accountability. Take the time to learn everything you can about the circumstances you are operating in.

Use this as an opportunity to build your knowledge and deepen your experience. Go and visit others who have navigated similar circumstances. Find the exceptional outcomes and learn from those who have conducted successful intelligence efforts themselves, ideally others who did so with a scope similar to yours.

I regularly teach CEOs in executive symposia that I design and run. In one year-long symposium I led my executives in an extensive conversation about leadership knowledge. It was the unanimous opinion of the group that the most valuable learning experiences occur when the stakes are the highest. This can happen one of two ways—either you find yourself out on a limb and suddenly have to marshal resources to save your own neck, or you proactively educate yourself so you are as well prepared as possible. Choose the latter when you can.

4. **Be transparent with your intelligence agents.** When a good deal is at risk, be explicit with your agents. Help them help you by being clear about what you need and why. Explain to them that risk is unusually high, there is a lot to be gained, and that important relationships are in conflict. Lay out the implications for the intelligence gathering you are

seeking. By being crystal clear you arm them with the knowledge they need to act in your best interest.

Each of these four tactics addresses a different aspect of due diligence. Creating a S.W.A.T. Team pulls in powerful expertise. Identifying legal parameters keeps you on the right side of the law. Taking responsibility for your education ensures you are acting in your own best interest in a high-risk situation. And being transparent with your agents makes it possible for them to be smart about how they are operating. Doing all four for maximum protection is appropriate in a high-risk situation.

Step 8. Format and Present Results for Maximum Impact

The presentation of results must aid you in making decisions about the issues that are foremost in your mind, advancing the cause of your organization to the greatest degree possible. Do not make the mistake of thinking that formatting is irrelevant to purpose.

Edward Tufte, an accomplished statistician and data-design expert, made famous the horrible documentation that failed to stop the launch of NASA's Challenger, which exploded in the second minute of its tenth mission in 1986.

Common knowledge says the technical cause of the Challenger disaster was a faulty part that allowed a plume of flame to impinge upon an external fuel tank, setting in motion a series of events that ultimately caused the tank to explode, the ship's structure to come apart, and the cabin with the crew plummeting down over 50,000 feet to hit the ocean's surface at about two hundred miles per hour.

But in his book[7] and one-man show Tufte displays the data that the scientists reviewed prior to launch. He includes a graph that shows the history of this kind of damage in chronological order. There is no discernable pattern. When Tufte simply rearranges the data display, organizing it by the surrounding temperature prior to lift-off, it becomes clear that launching the Challenger in these circumstances would have been a disaster as, tragically, it was.

Five Principles for Data Presentation: You must ensure that your data is well organized to be helpful — that key indicators influence the organizing principles. Here are five principles for data presentation that can help you keep your focus on the critical message in the data.

1. Use key indicators to organize presentation. These are the indicators that help you make decisions. If an indicator causes you to switch from one conclusion to another, it is key. Use these to categorize and display your data.

2. Accompany data with easy-to-understand narratives that explain their meaning.

3. Experiment with visual displays until you find natural correlations clearly expressed in easy-to-understand formats.

4. Include your intelligence agents in your initial presentations so they are on hand to answer questions.

5. Keep your first few presentations to a minimum of 10–20 minutes, providing a clear and simple overview of main results only. Let questions drive the granularity of the rest of the presentation. The concerns of the listeners can then drive the details presented and shape the thrust of the content provided.

These five principles will ensure that you communicate well with your intended audience. They will keep your findings intelligently organized and ensure your points are conveyed articulately. By following this method you will be most helpful to those who are relying on the information to make key decisions.

The eight steps of a business intelligence effort will ensure that you hit your target of providing valuable information to decision makers in the proper scope. Setting of goals gives the effort a compass to ensure it stays on track. The various techniques, including consulting a variety of information sources, conducting interviews with key stakeholders, and secret shopping, all surface critical information to inform the results. By iteratively sharing results and receiving direction, conducting due diligence, and doing an excellent job of presenting your results you will ensure that your bases are covered, decision makers are appropriately engaged, and you receive the direction you need to deliver on the promise of intelligence.

Use an External Provider for Intelligence

Throughout the previous eight steps I referred often to your intelligence agent. It is crucial that this person be an external provider to your organization, rather than a staff member. This is because the nature of the employer-employee relationship negates neutrality. This is a deal-breaker when it comes to intelligence. Employees will overlook questions and misrepresent results, not because they want to or feel compelled to. It will occur simply because they are embedded in the very entity at stake. This is true in all but the most insignificant of issues, in which case you don't need intelligence.

Even if by some miracle the person gathering the data manages to perform in a flawlessly unbiased fashion, the trust of both the respondents and recipients of the intelligence will be compromised. Don't do it. Hire an expert.

Six Guidelines for Working with an Intelligence Agent

1. Don't hire an expert who promises to be fully detached and neutral to your needs. You read that right and I am not contradicting my previous point. While it is critical that your agent is able to work outside the organization and gather information in an unbiased way, you also want the agent working for your success. All information has a context and your context is unambiguous: your success. Hire someone who understands that you are gathering information to help you succeed in the market and who will help you to choose the data and methods that best serve this goal.

2. Build in a due-diligence effort to understand and integrate the vision, mission, and objectives of your organization into the scope of work. In addition to working for your success, the agent must be well educated on where you are going, what you do, and your primary goals.

3. Demand the agent spends time with key staff members to develop a solid comprehension of recent history and developments, both

inside and outside the organization. This provides context that is critical to evaluating information. It is not extraneous or irrelevant.

4. Require that your provider conduct a comprehensive effort outside the organization to locate, understand, spell out, and address the blind spots that are part of every operation.

5. Insist on a working relationship that includes close contact with you and your team in an iterative fashion to share what is being learned and to correlate it with your goals.

6. Make clear the requirement to take direction continuously as your needs change, as they no doubt will due to circumstances and the awareness of new information from the intelligence effort. Many agents like to sign the contract, go off on their own, and then toss a report over the wall as they call it quits. This greatly devalues the potential return of a collaborative relationship. By taking into account the constant change that is part of business in the 21st century, you will be able to collaborate with your agent to produce intelligence that is more relevant and helpful to innovation.

With these six guidelines in place you are in a position to engage an expert who can help you secure the intelligence you can leverage to build powerful innovation initiatives. Such agents will operate outside your enterprise so they can bring you the data you need to hear, yet they will work toward your success, integrating your business needs into the spirit of their work.

Expert Input

KEN GARRISON OF STRATEGIC AND COMPETITIVE INTELLIGENCE PROFESSIONALS ON COMPETITIVE INTELLIGENCE

Ken Garrison is the former CEO of Strategic and Competitive Intelligence Professionals (SCIP.org), a global nonprofit serving professionals in the field of competitive intelligence. His first-hand experience with dozens of industry professionals including the luminaries in the field gives him insight into what it takes to make

Expert Input

a competitive intelligence effort succeed organizationally. I asked him to outline the conditions for creating a world-class intelligence environment. Here is what he told me.

A broad definition of competitive intelligence is the action of defining, gathering, analyzing, and distributing intelligence about products, customers, competitors, and any aspect of the environment needed to support executives and managers in making strategic decisions.

Competitive analysis looks at the market, its variables, adjacent markets, products, customers, and competitors, all so you can create a competitive edge. This is done over time so you can predict where trends may go as best you possibly can, and evaluate your ability to respond effectively.

In a changing world, leaders must realize that they are always a single event away from survival—they need to know what is on the horizon to stay relevant, competitive, and to win. Competitive intelligence provides information so you can answer questions like, "How do I make adjustments so I get my share of revenue growth, attractive markets, or expand my base?"

Many leaders do not know there are professionals who understand this, do it, and provide this kind of an edge. It is legal, ethical, and a professional discipline.

If you are going to create a world-class competitive intelligence program you have to have three things:

1. A strong personal understanding of what competitive intelligence is and how you can use it for business advantage. This understanding must reside in your chair. You are the CEO. If you do not get it, it will fail. When you understand it and own it, it becomes an extremely powerful tool.

2. A line item in the budget that you commit to. Do not bury it in marketing, research, development, or communications. Competitive intelligence makes a unique contribution. If you put it in one of those buckets, two things will happen: it will be

Expert Input

twisted by the office that runs it—that should instead be you, at the top—and it will be one of the first things cut when the office you put it in is forced to make tough decisions. Cutting competitive intelligence when times are rough is like saying we don't need to look out the front windshield of a car anymore when you are driving through a storm. That is when you most need to understand the trends and market.

3. You need a consistent presentation of results so you can see the work. You must have a way of disseminating your information, and your audience legitimately has the expectation that they are going to get something back.

As someone who surveys the entire field I see a significant shift when leaders begin taking competitive intelligence seriously. They realize an ad hoc effort will only get them so far. When a CEO chooses to do this in a modulated way over a period of time so they have a consistent set of facts and information flowing in, they achieve a new level of performance simply because they have better quality information, that is, data across time.

Intelligence increases the quality of strategic decision making by providing critical background information, as well as highlighting emerging possibilities that will impact your sector and your organization. Garrison has laid out the three elements that go into establishing a world-class effort, and it's clear from his insights that this is not something that most leaders do. Yet when they understand the benefits and begin to implement such a program the performance increases follow. That is why taking business intelligence seriously will put you ahead of much of the competition.

The Eight Elements of an Intelligence Contract

When you contract an intelligence agent, there are eight important elements to be made explicit in your agreement. You will find a sample contract in Appendix A.

The eight elements are

1. Situational summary
2. Objective
3. Measure of success
4. Value to the organization
5. Methodology and timeline
6. Joint accountabilities
7. Terms and conditions
8. Acceptance

A business intelligence contract will address each element. Without each, you are vulnerable to risk. The most common hazard is an incomplete, and therefore weak, intelligence effort; but other risks, such as a consulting relationship that goes astray, or wasted resources through flawed methodology or failures of accountability, can also result. I strongly recommend you build your working relationship with an intelligence provider on the sample contract I've provided, which includes these eight elements.

Situational Summary: This describes the current state and relevant conditions. It is not uncommon for it to be a short narrative that tells the story of what has happened to bring you to the point where business intelligence is required.

You want to capture everything that is relevant, but you want to keep it essential. The shorter, the better. It should be to the point. A situational summary may be one or two paragraphs, but no more. This is not an essay; it is a succinct background that makes clear your understanding of the context within which the intelligence effort is taking place.

Objective: A no-nonsense explanation of what exactly the intelligence effort will accomplish must be spelled out. The goals should be laid out concisely and in unambiguous terms.

You can expect to begin this section in a way something like, "Gather the intelligence required to . . ." This makes it plain why you are conducting intelligence. If the unexpected occurs (and it always does), this will be your compass. That is why you must be crystal clear about your objective.

Measure of Success: In this section you lay out how you will know the intelligence effort has succeeded. After these actions are carried out your effort will be complete because you will have met your objective.

Measures of success should be indisputable and objective. Any party should be able to easily evaluate the measures and provide an immediate and clear judgment as to whether or not they have been met.

Value to the Organization: It is important to articulate what the intelligence will do to improve the organization's situation. This explains the benefit to the organization's position in plain, uncomplicated terms that everyone can understand.

The value to the organization should make sense to every stakeholder: customer, partner, CEO, leaders, managers, everyone. The organization and its mission must be the ultimate beneficiary of the intelligence effort. This section expresses that in straightforward, clear-cut words.

Methodology and Timeline: The core activities must be spelled out in sequence. Here we see the actions the business intelligence agent will take and when they will be taken. It is not necessary to divulge every technique or explain in laborious detail exactly what the agent will be doing. As a professional he or she must have discretion to make additions or subtractions to the actual work, based upon meeting the objectives laid out above. However, you do need to make clear at a basic level what kind of activity is expected. By writing it out here, every party shares in the common understanding of what will take place.

Joint Accountabilities: Every good effort relies on the due diligence and good will participation of all parties to reach its potential. This is where you spell out what is expected of each.

This section generally includes assurance that all relevant documentation will be made available to the agent, the execution of nondisclosure agreements is expected, and that internally in your organization someone is appointed to assist the agent as needed.

Terms and Conditions: These are your arrangements, including fees, expenses, administration, and payment schedule. Generally, the fee is based on the project and never on the amount of time required. That way either party may suggest due diligence without worrying about a meter running.

Acceptance: It is important that all parties with fiscal or managerial oversight roles sign this document to demonstrate shared understanding of what will be done.

Include these eight elements in your contract with your intelligence agent and you should find that both the process and its ultimate product are solid and productive.

To truly set up your innovation efforts for success in the market, intelligence is a must. You cannot hope to provide new products and services that will do well in our complex marketplace without all the information you can get your hands on. You simply must learn all that can be known about your customers, the market, and your internal capabilities. How well you use intelligence will directly influence your success.

Success Rules

- Intelligence done right will provide valuable, legal, relevant data about customers, market conditions, and organizational capacity.
- The eight steps of an intelligence effort include defining scope, determining goals, conducting interviews, secret shopping, sharing findings, consulting sources, performing due diligence, and presenting results.

- Because the nature of the employer-employee relationship negates neutrality, you should hire an external agent to conduct your intelligence effort.
- To manage the agent's engagement, use the six guidelines presented in this chapter. Contract carefully (see Appendix A for a sample you can use as a template).

4

Shift Perspective

Shifting perspective is essential if you are going to get innovation right. Your current assumptions are constraining your thinking, whether you're aware of that fact or not. In this chapter I show you how to challenge those assumptions by applying four techniques for shifting perspective that should put you in a new relationship to everything you thought you knew. From this new perspective, you'll find it easier to innovate successfully.

Your clients, competitors, strategic partners, and industry observers each have a sense of the value your organization provides. But is it the same value proposition you and your marketing team have worked so hard to create and articulate? Maybe not!

Can you work your way around to seeing your business from their perspectives? You must try. Seeing your business from unconventional angles applies a powerful lens that brings into sharp focus how you can create new or better value for your clients and partners.

Working the Angles

Take a look at your business from a variety of angles. This includes seeing your operation as your customers and key partners see it. Seeing your enterprise as your clients and partners view it means understanding why they do business or join forces with you. If you do not know the *why* of their participation, you are severely handicapped when it comes to expanding the value they have come to rely on you to deliver. Working the angles will help you figure out what is nonnegotiable and what can change. That is information you need to put your enterprise in the best possible situation to innovate.

When you understand clearly why your customers come to you and why partners choose to work together with you, you are in a position to build on that knowledge. Then you can develop new products and services that make sense in their eyes. Such innovations are much more likely to be quickly received as a logical extension of your current offerings.

Shifting perspective keeps you from making silly mistakes and cutting away what is essential. If, for example, you are known for delivering the freshest produce, it would not make sense for you to cut your relationship with local farmers even when it costs more to do business with them—more than money is at stake.

When you know what your clients and partners believe is most valuable, your innovation program is more effective. You can focus your efforts on what interests your clients the most. For example, if they depend upon you to get them fresh fruit and vegetables every day, then providing them with fresh meat, too, will likely make you more valuable in their eyes.

When you see your operations from varying viewpoints you sometimes spot opportunities to parlay what you are doing today into a new field altogether. In that case, you are pivoting—a variation on shifting perspective that turns on what is good and solid to reach into new profitable endeavors.

Whether you are leveraging customer knowledge to deliver more or better value, or pivoting into position to offer entirely new value, you are mastering crucial innovation moves. All of these innovation moves are based upon your ability to shift perspective, see your business from multiple points of view, and take advantage of those angles for your benefit.

Pivoting for Success

When you can see the future in a way that differs dramatically from the prevailing viewpoint, you are in a position to pursue it even if others wonder what you are doing. This is what pursuing and leveraging inflection points is all about: discerning a future wave that can come into being but is not here yet, taking advantage of it, and achieving a decisive market victory as a result. Pivoting relies on your ability to see how present circumstances can best be used to your advantage. It can be a radical move, taking onlookers by surprise.

Philip Anschutz made such a pivot and generated a financial windfall early in his career. It was 1968 and he was a young man desperate to break into the oil business. Today he is a businessman with an estimated net worth of over $7 billion.[1]

Anschutz started in oil as a wildcatter. That means he was drilling on his own in obscure territory where there was no history of big oil finds. His initial efforts in the 1960s were unsuccessful, turning up one dry hole after another. He finally hit oil in Gillette, Wyoming, drilling under contract. Before he could relish his victory, a crisis he called "the most important single event" in his career took place.[2]

"About two o'clock in the morning the phone rang . . . . my drilling superintendent . . . . was calling to tell me that a well . . . had blown out and was out of control. In the oil business, that's an extremely serious and dangerous thing . . . . careers can be ended and people hurt physically, as well as financially."[3]

Anschutz flew out to visit the well and found it spewing haphazardly because they had hit oil earlier than anticipated. He put a crew together and they worked around the clock for a day and a half to get it to stop gushing—without success. When he got back to his hotel the next day he saw his well on the news. Now it was on fire.

What he did next defied expectation. He flew back and negotiated with his partner to obtain more owner interest in return for taking on total liability and ownership of the flaming well. Their deal was drawn up on a bar room tablecloth. He went on to lease all the oil and gas rights associated with his discovery.

He promised full payment within 30 days even though he did not yet have the money. He raised the money by first approaching banks and then by selling a portion of his interest in the well. But, you may wonder, what about the fire?!

Anschutz had heard that Universal Studios was making a movie starring John Wayne called *Hellfighters* about the legendary oil-field fire fighter, Red Adair. Adair had become a worldwide fire fighting celebrity in 1962 when he successfully put out a gas fire in Algeria nicknamed the Devil's Cigarette Lighter. The Algerian conflagration had burned continuously for over five months with a 450 foot plume at its peak. Adair's success landed him on the cover of *Life Magazine*.

Anschutz had already approached Adair to put out his fire once, but the fire fighter had refused because of financial risk. He knew Anschutz was young and short of funds so he wanted to be paid in advance. The first time he approached Adair, Anschutz had no money, so no deal was reached.

Anschutz called Universal Studios and told them they could film Adair putting out his fire for $100,000. They went for it. The studio cut a check and Anschutz used the initial payment to hire Adair while pocketing the rest as profit. The footage of Anschutz's rig being put out by Adair is in the movie.

Anschutz forged forward through circumstances most people would have run from, turned them to his advantage, and emerged victorious. It was an ordeal, no doubt. The average person would have clutched.

Anschutz himself admits he entertained failure. In an interview he remarked that after he made his deal, he saw the flames of his destroyed rig shooting hundreds of feet in the air from a hundred miles away in an airplane. He said to himself, "This is the end. I'll never be able to overcome all this."[4] But he did.

Shifting his perspective to an unconventional viewpoint allowed Anschutz to see a business opportunity where it was not apparent to others. When it seemed circumstances were failing him, he was able to focus on opportunity and pivot toward it.

The assumptions we have about what is possible and how the world works can work for us or against us. They are the building blocks we use to assemble all the options we imagine are achievable.

Innovation requires breaking away from the accepted possibilities in order to create something new. An essential skill required to shift perspective in this way is the ability to intentionally change your assumptions.

Change Your Assumptions

All beliefs are built upon a set of assumptions. Our assumptions are the elements we use to construct new ideas in our imagination, and they constrain us to what we readily accept and believe is possible. When those assumptions change, there is a corresponding effect that changes what we imagine and then in turn what we create.

For example, when we think about improving the computer interface, most of us assume we need to touch the machine through the keyboard, screen, some kind of pad, or be in a position to speak into a microphone. That's built on the assumption that interacting with the computer requires our initiating contact and articulating our commands through text or voice.

But today there are products on the market that watch you and respond to your movement. Soon it will be commonplace to interact with computers using face and gesture, some of the most nuanced and intricate forms of human communication. Perhaps you are already thinking of computers that anticipate your needs based on the expression on your face, compose music based on detailed hand movements, or manipulate data as depicted in Hollywood's futuristic thrillers. We are used to computers watching us when we go to the hospital and get hooked up to a machine. We know about computers that observe and adjust traffic flow. But owning a computer that is watching our face, our body, and learning to interpret our movements is not common yet.

As long as your marketplace behaves consistently — customers experience uniform pressures, industries remain stable, competition rises and falls in slow waves, and the ways you earn money are straightforward — there is no real push to question these basic assumptions. Innovation does not have the same importance in a stable environment.

But we know that today's environment is not stable. In fact, it is changing rapidly. So questioning basic assumptions about the rules of the game is necessary. Changing assumptions opens new opportunities for innovation.

Seeing things in unconventional ways allows us to see business opportunities where they were not apparent before. Then we can innovate, take advantage of them, and generate the inflection points that reflect our success in the market.

Four Techniques for Shifting Perspective

I have identified four techniques you can use to achieve a change in viewpoint that allows you to spot real options for innovation:

1. Isolate and examine the steps in your value chain.
2. Become your competition.
3. Seek out and highlight your weak spots.
4. Look to creative deviants for inspiration.

Each technique can help you shift perspective toward new innovations, the kind that drive positive inflection points. Let's zoom in for a detailed examination of each.

Isolate and Examine the Steps in Your Value Chain

The *value chain* is a sequence of events that takes place inside your business unit, each of which adds value to your products or services. An example helps illustrate this concept.

An intelligence firm specializes in providing reports to companies in the metals industries. The reports are intended to help recipients maximize sales and profitability. These reports include data for shipments, inventory, financial benchmarking, and operational benchmarking within the metal distribution industry.

First the firm interviews customers in a process designed to help them understand the nuances that determine profitability for each of its clients' business models. Then these interviews are translated into data requirements; that is, the firm determines what data would make a competitive difference for the customer. Next the firm pulls data together and correlates it through a computer program.

A small team of economists specializing in the metal sectors analyzes the correlated data. After the specialists conduct their analysis, they construct a numerical report. The economists write a narrative for the numerical report designed to address particular questions, issues, and needs of the firm's clients.

The firm provides the resulting document to the client. Following delivery, a scheduled phone call takes place to understand what aspects of the document proved most valuable. Whenever possible the value is quantified. Requests are gathered from each client on a monthly basis to improve the document and change it to suit current client needs.

Each of these is a step in the value chain. Here they are again, summarized for brevity:

1. Client interview takes place
2. Interview yields client data requirements
3. Data is gathered
4. Data is correlated.
5. Correlated data is analyzed by industry economists
6. Numerical report is constructed
7. Narrative is created
8. Combined document is provided to client
9. Follow up interview takes place to gather new requirements and refine

In each of the nine steps, the intelligence firm adds value. To the extent that they do a better or worse job at each stage, they generate more or less value at that juncture. Each one of these steps can be isolated and examined for quality of execution, the factors that contribute to quality of execution, and the results used to look at your business from a new angle.

For example, let's take a look at step #2, "interview yields client data requirements."

How well is it executed? Is it done mindlessly using a formula that is the same from client to client, or is it done thoughtfully in a process that carefully considers each client? Is the process done in a way that the analysts seek only to cover the basics, or do they operate with a mandate to go the extra yard and think as if they were the client?

What factors contribute to the quality of execution? Are industry experts consulted or is it a team of technology geeks who know nothing about metals? Is it done in a hurry to meet deadline and avoid over-time or is there a strong spirit of due diligence that compels people to stay late if needed to create a superior product? The answers to these questions provide insight into improving the process and establishing a level of excellence not yet achieved, perhaps even a key to becoming an industry leader.

As the data requirement process is opened up and examined in detail, new perspectives surface that yield opportunities for innovation. By breaking down the steps of your value chain, you can do a comprehensive review of each and every way you add value to your products and services. These activities each become a microworld, and the qualities that make them more or less successful can add information that will help you shift your perspective, taking more into consideration that will help you innovate successfully.

Become Your Competition

Take a day with your senior leadership and put together a plan of attack to take down your business. Identify the weak points. Get into it and have fun.

Then take it to another level of seriousness. Instead of attacking your program generally, don the guise of your most threatening competitors. Pretend you are their senior strategy team. Talk about your firm's weaknesses from your competitors' positions of strength.

It takes some guts to do this, as the conversation is likely to violate what is considered politically correct, naming your weaknesses and speaking of them openly as if you can exploit them. But the reward is significant. You'd better believe this is exactly the kind of conversation that takes place in the conference rooms of your competition.

As you are going through this process there are likely to be moments when the mood changes and people really let go. This is the time to be taking notes. I suggest recording the event with an audio recorder so you are not distracted by taking notes. You can give yourself to the role play and review the recording later to mine it for gems. It is likely that important facts and perspectives will emerge, those that are normally kept in abeyance.

Consider how these perspectives, once out in the open, might be used to your advantage. If you understand the intentions of those who want to take over your space, what might you do differently as a matter of course?

The answer to this question can fuel important innovations, break-throughs that secure market share or fortify a tenuous position. Perspectives that arise as you take on the motives and persona of your competition are not often welcome, but brought in with the right attitude they can add real value.

Seek Out and Highlight Weak Spots

This activity, too, can open up taboos and provide the kind of medicine that makes you stronger and more robust in the market. Spend some time questioning the unquestionable. Here you do not limit yourself to competition but explore all aspects of weakness — your own and your clients'.

I like to look for three weak points:

1. Changing circumstances
2. Educational deficiencies
3. Superstitions

Changing Circumstances   Sometimes developing or changing circumstances can collide with current work. For example, if you are developing an initiative to go to Capitol Hill and lobby for a policy change in your field, but there is a groundswell of support gathering in the public media that would call for the polar opposite of your effort, you may be opening your organization up to criticism and thereby weakening it. Or if you are embarking on a program to provide a new form of consumer financing just as the market is showing signs that it may sour due to bad press, this change in circumstances could derail your success. If you go forward, you have to be prepared to steer through a storm.

Educational Deficiencies   Educational deficiencies betray a lack of understanding that could undermine your success. For instance, you have an advanced computer modeling system that uses fiber optics to scan and map the image of an underground oil well but your current portfolio of clients are averse to anything that relies on fiber optics. That your clients prefer their standard modeling techniques, even though your product is test-proven superior, is an educational deficiency. You need to educate them to have a shot at success.

Superstition   Superstition covers anything that is irrational but prevalent among your customers. It frankly does not matter that it is irrational, because it has the power to interfere with your success and that is what counts. Maybe you have a new product that you want to introduce in another country, but it violates a cultural taboo. I remember working on a technology project in an international organization and we wanted to use an owl as our logo. After a bit of research we discovered that the owl was considered a well-known sign of stupidity among a critical constituency in parts of China. We got a different logo. If we had not been willing to shift our perspective it could have been the end of our otherwise successful project.

Exploring each of these potential weaknesses can reveal unique angles that highlight valuable opportunity, and they are often found in the very places where you are vulnerable. Not only might exploring these perspectives allow you to bolster your programs where you need it most, but they can become sources of strength.

Look to Creative Deviants

Creative deviants are people who come up with inventive ways to circumvent the norm. In the Introduction I described the World Bank as at first toxic to professional communities, wiping them out where they surfaced. Yet there were five that we discovered that managed to eek out an existence, and one in particular that was robust. The leader was a creative deviant. He had come up with some very imaginative ways to build community inside our organization despite its proclivity to destroy them.

Creative deviants provide valuable information, showing how the system can be worked to achieve their ends. When their goals are constructive, they have beneficial lessons to teach.

Somewhere among the group of people you turn to for advice and inspiration you should include a few creative deviants. These are the people who can bang on your brain with thinking so far outside your box it redefines the meaning of "box." These people, through their unconventional outlooks, seed innovation wherever they go.

Let me return to the World Bank knowledge management story again to show how a creative deviant helped us find our way. Remember, we realized early on in our initiative that communities were the key to our success. So we had to figure out a way to grow communities across our organization and around the world if we were to be successful.

We tracked down those few groups that had figured out how to survive in our organization and discovered a project manager who specialized in highways—and he had the key. In addition to being a recognized world-class thought leader in his field he was a social marvel. These days many professionals are active socially, but at the World Bank in the early 1990s taking an interest in social activity was a rarity.

He brokered knowledge between individuals. As an example, in his travels he might come across someone struggling with keeping pavement from dissolving in the Amazon jungle and another having success with asphalt in high humidity conditions in a lab in Switzerland. He would introduce the two and often be present when they actually met. He was known for this kind of matchmaking.

He brought people together all the time, arranging for groups to meet and discuss critical issues at gatherings large and small. He handed out lists of publications and contact information for experts in the field. Pre-computer he used a three-ring binder. Then he went to diskettes. Then it was email. The technology was always secondary to the aim, which was to connect all the experts in his field. I call him a *social architect*, because he designed gatherings and engineered introductions. At the time this was a deviation from the World Bank norm. Most people worked in isolation or among small groups but did not take on the responsibility of networking, welcoming newcomers, and putting on events. He did. He showed us the way toward an inflection point we never would have seen on our own. Because of him the highway group had been a successful community inside the World Bank for years before we came along.

Who in your operation is succeeding despite the odds? What magic are they mixing that is allowing them to get traction? What unorthodox behavior getting stellar results are they exhibiting? Answer these questions and you will come upon unconventional ways of working that may lead to more widespread success.

ROGER MARTIN OF THE UNIVERSITY OF TORONTO'S JOSEPH L. ROTMAN SCHOOL OF MANAGEMENT ON THINKING DIFFERENTLY

Roger Martin was selected as the sixth top management thinker in the world 2011.[5] He is the dean of the Joseph L. Rotman School of Management at the University of Toronto and serves as a counselor to senior executives through his firm, Strategic Choice Architecture. He is the author of numerous books. Many of his superb articles are available for free on his website, www.RogerLMartin.com. I asked Martin for his thoughts on powering innovation through unconventional thinking.

Leaders are constrained only by the fear of how much they will have to change to take into account what they find out. With respect to customers, lots of companies don't want to turn over rocks for fear of what they'll find underneath them.

The fear is that they will have to radically restructure their organizations. They worry that if they go and sit with the customers and find out customers actually don't really like their product the way they deliver it, they may have to change it in a radical way. Change tends to be scary until you have done a significant amount of it.

Do we cross over a threshold where we start to get excited by it?

Certainly, there are companies that say, "Consumers are changing all the time. We have to keep updating ourselves and changing with them. We are good at that. We'll do it. That does not make us worry."

But there are others that have not had the practice of changing and having things turn out fine. It's often either an upward or downward spiral. On the one hand, if you're proactive and you change before you have to change, then you will likely have enough time to do it right. You can be successful and it feels good.

If instead you stay constant, hoping that you don't have to change, and wait until the last minute to change, then you are forced to change really quickly. Then it does feel as though change is painful, dangerous, and worrisome.

It is a deep human desire to not be scared by things. This is because when you're scared your brain doesn't reason well. Our fight-or-flight mechanism takes over and messes up our brain.

Your work focuses on helping managers and leaders think about the world in different ways. It sounds like a skill set that leaders must develop has to do with operating without fear at the frontier of business, and that's an uncertain place.

I think that's right. And really the question is, are they going to let themselves be so fearful they fall into the flight-or-fight mode or will they be able to step back and assess the situation as not so horrible and torturous and dangerous — and ask, "What can I do to make things better?"

This is why my focus is on giving managers tools for understanding innovation and design and strategy and change. With tools they will be less afraid.

We must give people tools to help them feel calm and empowered when facing tricky and difficult situations. If we can succeed

Expert Input

on that front we will contribute to better decisions being made, and that will result in a better world.

One of the messages that Martin's work conveys to me is that people can become not just accepting but also actively desirous of change. Those who experience initial successes by being proactive rather than reactive catch an updraft that feels good to ride—even if it carries them toward a frontier where fear is a more conventional reaction.

As these examples make clear, the way to shift perspective is to deploy the four techniques I've described. Analyze your value chain in the greatest detail possible; step into the perspective of your competition and play your new role to the hilt; go after your weak spots; and learn from creative deviants. Execute well on these four and you are sure to identify critical assumptions you can change to pivot toward success.

A New Way of Seeing

Once you are able to see things in an unconventional way should you act on every new perspective you find? No—because not every business opportunity is worth pursuing, even when the idea behind it is inherently sound.

Most organizations' fundamental objective can be summed up in two words: *targeted growth*. When you consider the innovations you might pursue, you must ensure they align with your strategic objectives—most likely targeted growth—or you risk undertaking innovation that pulls your organization off purpose. I recommend a four-step process to assure that your innovations align with strategy:

1. Identify new assumptions that differ from those you currently hold (using the techniques I've described).
2. Explore scenarios, projecting the results you anticipate if you adopted one or more of these assumptions.

3. Incorporate the assumptions that would lead to increased value that is aligned with your organization's strategy and goals.
4. Develop innovations that spring from the new assumptions.

Once you have that match of new assumptions and new innovations, you are on your way to pursuing and leveraging a positive inflection point.

Viewing your world from a different angle requires getting out of your own way, avoiding your proclivities, and questioning the assumptions that likely have aided your success up to this point. It is not an easy task, but it is a skill all leaders must master if they want to innovate and reach levels beyond their current success.

Success Rules

- Learn to see the value your organization provides from a variety of angles. Never mind what you believe — what do clients and strategic partners believe is most valuable?
- An unconventional perspective will help you identify opportunities to pivot into a positive inflection point that will drive success.
- In today's unstable environment, questioning basic assumptions leads to new opportunities for innovation.
- To shift your perspective, step out of your leadership role and listen to your employees, partners, and customers.
- Add these techniques for shifting perspective to your toolbox: examine your value chain, think like your competition, seek out weak spots, and look to creative deviants for inspiration.
- Identify new assumptions springing from your perspective shift and develop the innovations that spring from those new assumptions.

Exploit Disruption

Disruption. It can come from anywhere. If ignored or mis-
managed, it throws business into disarray. But what if you
could take the forces behind these intrusions and turn them
to your advantage? That's what the masters do. Instead of being waylaid
by adverse conditions, they use them to get the upper hand. You can
and you must become an expert in exploiting disruptions. Don't fight
change but use it to your advantage.

Market fluctuations are normal, including fast, painful declines and
long, confusing morasses. Rapid fluctuations are particularly disruptive.
The market plunges, a sexy new competitor moves into your space,
technology changes too fast to keep pace, customer expectations slam
you. We've all been there. Welcome to life in the 21st century.

Innovation can be thought of as intentional evolution. It is the
deliberate and successful adaptation to circumstance that generates
enough value to justify the investment. It is about taking advantage of
disruption — and it is not an accident. It is a mind-set and set of skills
to develop, cultivate, and master.

Sure, we have all heard the great stories of mistakes turned to
great profits, like when Will Kellogg took some stale wheat in 1894 and
tried to make dough but got flakes instead. But that mistake was not
their innovation. The innovation took place 12 years later when, after
much experimentation, they decided to add sugar and mass market the
flakes. That's when they started the Battle Creek Toasted Corn Flake

Company,[1] introducing the first batch of Kellogg's Corn Flakes®.[2] And it didn't stop there.

Seventy-seven years later cereal had bottomed out as a children's food. These are the kind of adverse conditions I speak of. In response the Kellogg Company took it upon itself to convince adult America that cereal was nutritional and easy to eat. They stepped into the storm instead of away from it as so many others were inclined to do. They were successful and moved cereal from a $3.7 billion industry in 1983 to $5.4 billion in 1988.[3] This inflection point did not happen by accident. It came as a result of actions born of intense will to succeed in a challenging marketplace.

One of the ways innovation works is by making full use of disruption to create a superior advantage. Gathering intelligence (as described in Chapter 3) contributes to your ability to exploit disruption. It does this by identifying disruptions before they break, giving you advance notice and time to prepare.

Innovation can produce benefits that include enhanced productivity, improved efficiencies, greater profits, increased market share, and exceptional growth in value. Through these kinds of breakthroughs organizations strengthen and improve their positions. They might do this through increasing short-term gains, improving long-term survival, or both. Either way threats are minimized, eliminated or evaded. At its best innovation turns disruptive circumstances into prominence, power, and advantage.

The Four Forces of Disruption

I've identified four forces of disruption, any or all of which can reorganize the playing field rapidly or muddy it interminably:

1. Customers are facing challenges.
2. Industries are upending.
3. Competition is fierce.
4. New business models are proliferating.

Understand each and you can turn them to your advantage. Misunderstand, and you will miss out on potential opportunities, fall behind in a changing marketplace, or worse yet, be crushed as the competition rolls right on over you. Each force deserves a closer examination.

Customers Are Facing Challenges

A tough economy impacts your clients just as it impacts you. Many leaders don't pay attention to this. Instead, when change hits and the status quo is threatened, they get so focused on their own survival that they miss the very key to making it through: their own clients.

Your customers have their own businesses to run. Many have demanding, difficult finances; cash flow is frequently a problem even for very successful businesses. As a result they may be inspecting costs more thoroughly, aggressively shaving expenses where they can, becoming increasingly interested in where they can commoditize, and changing their buying habits accordingly. They are learning how to do things for themselves that they used to pay for and demanding more from the people who serve them whenever possible.

Further, due to the stress created by this turmoil, some customers are making poor or short-sighted decisions, thus making them difficult to serve. They slash services to save money and step free of trusted relationships. It's a set of moves motivated by fear. Fear-based decisions may solve some problems in the short term but they do not sustain a long-term effort. As a result these imprudent tactics, initially providing relief, turn out to create even more challenges.

Industries Are Upending

Technology is rolling out one breakthrough after another. This will not stop. All signs indicate that we are only beginning to experience the transformations technology can enable. These technology advances affect individual businesses and the infrastructure that connects them. As more advances roll out, there will be massive disruptions as industries struggle to build the infrastructure required to accommodate new technology.

It is difficult to keep up with the investment in new technology that is often required just for the privilege of competing. I did some work in the printing equipment industry in 2010. That same year the iPad launched and sold over 14 million units. It was a game changer, because it dramatically hastened consumers' move from paper to screens, seriously affecting publishers of magazines and newspapers. As a result many dollars that had been dedicated to print were reallocated to electronic publications, causing havoc among those who operated printing equipment as a core revenue source. But that was not the only front on which the printing industry faced dramatic change.

This was also a time during which the printing industry was facing the challenge of continued movement from analog printing equipment to digital presses. Many owners of small print shops were used to buying equipment that cost $2–6 million. The financing they received allowed them ten years or more to pay it off. Now new technologies are being released so fast they cannot pay the machines off before they need the next press essential to compete and win customers. As a result these small, privately held shops are folding or getting bought up by bigger players. The printing equipment industry is not alone in this challenge of financing major purchases in a collapsing window for payback.

Then there is the need to acquire talent and educate employees so new capabilities can be leveraged. Without the right people, how can you hope to understand and exploit the opportunities each technology breakthrough brings to your industry?

Competition Is Fierce

Stalwart monoliths are toppling and being replaced by a new generation of market players. Deloitte reports, "The 'topple rate' at which big companies lose their leadership positions has more than doubled, suggesting that 'winners' have increasingly precarious positions."[4] Further, "Competitive intensity is increasing as barriers to entry and movement erode under the influence of digital infrastructure and public policy."[5]

Those who understand the new marketplace rise to prominence on a scale more massive and at a speed faster than ever possible before. Salesforce.com, Apple, and Google are just a few of the many companies that made the ascent to market dominance suddenly, their positive inflection points taking place over a span of months rather than years.

When competition invades your sector you have to be ready to learn and move faster than ever before.

New Business Models Are Proliferating

The ways to generate profitable revenue are evolving rapidly. With the advent of new products, services, and technologies, entrepreneurs and business leaders are creating breakthrough revenue generators leaving tried-and-true methods in the dust or the ditch.

I recall years ago walking into my local Apple store to pick up a pair of headphones and after the purchase the clerk asked if I wanted my receipt emailed. "Sure," I said and felt a little uncomfortable as I walked out of the store sans receipt in hand. But it was cool. I had a feeling of being in a new world.

In June 2012 the same clerk told me I could now pay for my purchases with an app on my iPhone. No need to deal with the cash register at all. I pick up the product, scan it myself, and pay electronically without any store staff interaction. When I am in the store I feel like I am on the edge of consumer experience, and I'll pay extra for that. That's an example of a new business model: customers paying for a do-it-yourself, unsupervised (except for the usual security surveillance), cashless interaction.

But my experience is only one facet of that inflection point. The capacity for customers to provide their own checkout experience has been in the works for decades. Today it has shifted out of the plateau of a Vertical Climb inflection point and is moving into dramatic ascent. It is lowering retail operation costs, creating new marketing opportunities at point of sale, increasing trust in brands, and accelerating the speed of commerce.

This is just one example of a new business model. These models are everywhere, generating value and opening up new options for customers, delivering cool new things and services they want and will pay for while leading them away from those who are providing traditional offerings.

Here is a summary of the forces of disruption:

The Four Forces of Disruption

1. Customers are facing challenges.
    a. Clients are demanding more.
    b. Some are stressed, making poor, short-sighted decisions.
    c. Customers are inspecting costs, aggressively shaving expenses.

2. Industries are upending.
    a. Technology breakthroughs are incessant.
    b. Employees must be educated to take advantage of new capabilities.
    c. Businesses find it challenging to keep up with the investments required to compete.

3. Competition is fierce.
    a. Stalwart monoliths are toppling.
    b. New contenders are rising to prominence faster than ever.
    c. Faster, more effective responses are required.

4. New business models are emerging.
    a. New products and services continuously entice clients to shop elsewhere.
    b. New ways of generating value attract your customers.
    c. Breakthrough revenue generators roll over traditional operations.

Turn Turmoil to Advantage

Being innovative in this environment means taking the adverse conditions and finding ways to use their momentum to your advantage. Imagine if you could take all the frustration and time spent coping with disruptions and instead literally harness their movement and direction to fuel your growth. Wouldn't that be better? That's what exploiting disruption can do for you. But, it requires an intentional shift in mind-set and a working knowledge of some critical tactics.

You will have to learn to shift your focus from being aggravated by intrusions to examining them for the opportunities within. You have to pull back on your natural and all-too-human inclination to be bothered by what is interfering with your intentions. Instead apply your acumen. Identify new factors that can work to your advantage.

Embracing disruption is a discipline that flies against prevailing attitudes and day-to-day proclivities. But, once mastered, the payoff is significant—a powerful turnaround that can propel your business forward instead of stalling you out or putting you in reverse.

Each of the points listed in the preceding section could potentially become an area in which you can innovate. Let's look at the first force of disruption in more detail, supported by examples.

When Customers Are Facing Challenges...

In each instance you are taking the adversity—your customers' situation—and using it to increase your advantage and form tighter relationships with your patrons.

Let me illustrate with a story. I worked recently with the CEO of a retirement community who was overhauling her systems to provide care that was customer-centric, differentiating it from competitors where care was institution-centric. For example, the CEO changed the way meals were served so residents could eat whatever and whenever they wanted instead of interrupting the residents' schedule (often waking them up) and taking them to the cafeteria early so the predetermined menu could be served efficiently. Instead, she directed her organization to design a flexible food service operation and provide short-order cooks who could fill a wide variety of meal orders.

This resident-centric approach extended through every aspect of operation from medical care to room decorations. The CEO, CFO, and senior management team designed business processes and financial systems to support this approach. They worked with vendors,

Table 5.1 Turning Your Customers' Challenges to Advantage

When clients demand more from you, you have an invitation to ...	Step into a tighter relationship with them.
	Ask for more data in return, to increase your ability to serve them.
	Customize your relationship.
If you see customers making short-sighted decisions, you can ...	Educate them.
	Help them weigh costs to benefits.
	Become proactive by improving the quality of their choices.
When customers begin inspecting costs more closely, dramatically and forcefully cutting expenses, you can ...	Provide services to help them control costs.
	Provide tools (checklists, white papers, templates) to optimize their overhead.
	Help them choose value-based or performance-based options that lead to the greatest advantage for them.

policymakers, and other partners so they, too, would contribute to the resident-centric way of doing business.

Of course, rising care costs were a concern to residents and their families who were managing expenses. The stress associated with placing a loved one in an institution for long-term care along with financial pressures made it difficult for the families to think straight and choose the right options. This disruption would unsettle most CEOs attempting to build a resident-centric model, knowing the associated costs incurred in such a profound change. But this CEO set up specialized services to provide a low-stress environment where clients could review the many options and choose those that fit their budget while creating the optimal living experience, working together with her customers to find the sweet spot where their budget met the new offerings.

This meant a shift away from focusing first on cost (typical of other facilities) and toward a strategy that started with the resident in mind (consistent with the overall thrust of her work). The result was a brand that grew beyond the state's borders and attracted families and residents across the nation.

The point of my story is that you must study the stresses and challenges, take them into consideration, and use them to innovate. Often the very force that is disrupting your business is pointing to innovation that has the power to take you through a positive inflection point.

Turning turmoil to your advantage is a basic way to innovate. It meets disruption with a desire to uncover and take advantage of the opportunity embedded in adverse conditions. By consistently applying this approach you will begin to see that the same circumstances that are causing discomfort are also midwifing the future.

When Industries Are Upending . . .

In every one of the instances just mentioned you are responding to rapid change across an entire industry. These are market forces bigger than any one player can control. While companies contribute to their momentum, they sweep through like forces of nature, dramatically shifting the playing field. If you get in their way you can be drowned or crushed. But if you understand their direction and dynamics, you can actually move into alignment and use them to propel you on to new heights.

I had an opportunity to work with a CEO, Mike Panaggio, who shifted his relationship with print technology to take advantage of its unceasing advances. His enterprise has experienced remarkable growth as a result, adding $75 million over 10 years to his total valuation of over $100 million as of this writing.[6]

Panaggio is founder and chairman of DME Holdings, LLC. He began his career in the early 1980s providing clients with marketing expertise and soon entered the print business to control costs and quality. But over time printing has become one of the most challenging businesses in which to compete, due to the constant onslaught of new and better technology.

Table 5.2   Turning Industry Upheaval to Advantage

As breakthroughs continuously emerge . . .	Change your relationship to the technology; for example, instead of attempting to master a tool, master the process of integrating new tools.
	Align your business model and brand with new technology that has demonstrated profitability.
	Become expert in the changes hitting your industry; publish and establish yourself as an industry leader in knowledge.
When employees lack the skills to take advantage of new capabilities . . .	Bring in thought leaders to show them the benefits; prize expertise in new skill sets as part of your corporate culture.
	Shift professional development opportunities toward new technologies and make the training a priority; reward demonstrated advanced skill with raises.
	Hire talent that knows how to capitalize on new capabilities and set them up to mentor others.
When challenged by the investments required to compete . . .	Outsource costly resources and market your newfound flexibility.
	Create new partnerships to access emerging tools and services, then expand through your partners' markets.
	Market to clients who have made the investment and need help capturing ROI.

Panaggio says,

As digitization took over in the 2000s, I quickly realized I was not in the print business. I was not attached to those machines. My job was *not* to sell more print. I was in the business of helping my customers achieve sustainable, profitable revenue growth.

As a result of this shift in focus, I sold off most of my machines and relentlessly did whatever it took to get results for my customers. I grew my ability to handle multiple platforms, all technologies. Honestly, it was secondary to my primary goal. My mantra is sustainable, profitable revenue growth.

DME's services now include production, video, telephony, Internet, office, and warehouse facilities as well as printing. My office has expanded to an 11 acre facility. I do not rely on any one piece of technology, but instead I work with my customers to create success. I will work with whatever technology suits that end. If I don't have it, it doesn't slow me down. In fact, it sometimes speeds me up! I don't have to maintain it — I just need to use it.[7]

Panaggio handled the industry turmoil by distancing himself from the technology and getting closer to his customers' primary concern. As a result he was able to find ways to use any technology they needed without the overhead of maintaining it.

As industries change, so do our relationship to them. By staying closer to customers than our chosen field, we can navigate the turbulence and build even more value where it counts.

When Competition Is Fierce...

This disruption is like combat. It requires its own strategies that are not useful in peacetime. From the get-go you know there are competitors strategizing to take you down. Opportunities can open up very fast — as can risks. Planning and preparation is critical, but as they say, "no battle plan survives contact with the enemy." This means that in the heat of competition you will face unanticipated threats and respond creatively in ways you could not know in advance.

Table 5.3   Turning Competition to Advantage

When stalwart giants come tumbling down . . .	New market space opens up in their absence.
	New partners arise, often offering better services, products, and/or terms of sale and support.
	As one organization falls, another rises, highlighting valuable market trends.
When new contenders take over market space quickly . . .	They bring with them a spate of opportunities for complementary offerings.
	New chances for partnerships and alliances open up.
	The market pecking order shifts and you have an opportunity to upgrade your position.
As faster, more effective responses are required, you can . . .	Specialize in speed as a way to rise to the top.
	Build your capacity to respond as a core competence.
	Provide tools that accelerate education and improve response potency for your most important partners as a way to reinforce your team's advance.

Be ready to pivot from your carefully laid plans to take advantage of circumstances arising from engagement with competitors. For example, you could spot an overlooked need for a complementary product or service in a competitor's move or find an opportunity for an unexpected strategic alliance.

Allies make or break success. New partnerships often emerge, helping each to benefit from the others' unique position and assets. As an illustration, I came across a unique tactic for a behemoth to increase its reach while providing resources to myriad smaller players.

Earlier I mentioned my conversation with the executive vice president of a Fortune 5 company during the difficult market of 2010. In his industry well-known giants were losing market share while entrepreneurs were cooking up solutions on smaller scales. He explained to me that although his research and development (R&D) shop was heavily invested with great minds and a large budget, his organization was not nimble. His was the battleship that could not turn quickly or change directions to capitalize on opportunity even though they could often see it.

To compensate, he was actively building relationships with many smaller organizations that were agile, able to change position and pursue new developments quickly. When something novel popped up on the horizon he asked them to investigate, sometimes funding their efforts. If they found something worth exploring, they would report back and possibly begin developing it with assistance from the larger company.

In this way he got the best of both worlds: a major R&D effort and a fleet of agents actively checking out new developments that popped up far afield. They in return got the benefit of his investments and possibly a share in a joint project at a scale they could not afford to fund.

When competition is fierce, opportunistic alliances provide the resources it takes to be ambitious beyond your normal reach. Alliances can fortify giants, open opportunity for smaller players, and enable faster, more effective responses for everyone.

In this case strategic alliances not only helped the VP take advantage of the mobility, nimbleness, and speed that smaller operations have at their disposal, it provided him with insight on emerging business models that he would soon be competing with.

When New Business Models Are Emerging...

This force of disruption can feel very threatening. New business models reframe existing markets and cast traditional offerings as obsolete. However, that reframing never dominates the entire market. When a new way of doing things sweeps along, changing the landscape, there

Table 5.4   Turning the Rise of New Business Models to Advantage

When your clients are being enticed away by the never-ending parade of the new, you can . . .	Use others' new models as a continuous opportunity to reframe your value. Take advantage of their hard work, failures, and lessons to leapfrog to a new and better model yourself.
	Stand as a contrarian, even marketing the value of tradition when advantageous. Sometimes new developments leave very large segments of the population behind and successful businesses can be built around catering to their needs.
	Find a way to improve on your competitors' sexiest innovation that enhances your brand.
When new forms of value generation capture clients, you have opportunity to . . .	Be aggressive and shift your position dramatically. This can be the time to invest in a bold move (as long as you have done your due diligence collecting intelligence as covered in Chapter Three).
	Ride the wave; create your own version of the same. Identify the new value proposition your competitor has introduced and transpose it to your market.
	Find a complementary offering that takes advantage of the competition's offering. When Apple came out with the iPad, Amazon developed a Kindle app that could run on the iPad.
When breakthrough revenue generators trump traditional operations . . .	Take a clue from the victors and adopt new practices.
	Create a variation on the theme for an attractive market segment.
	Carry the new model into as yet unexploited territory.

are always groups of customers who do not like the changes or are genuinely unaffected by them.

For every early adopter who must try the next new thing, there is a latecomer who resists change and clings hard to tradition. You have a choice. You can adopt and adapt the new ways of working, focus your business on those who are not yet part of the new wave, or if you have the bandwidth widen your offerings to serve both.

If the timing of an emerging business model is wrong for you, buy time by serving those unaffected by that inflection point. By focusing on serving latecomers and nonadopters, you can sometimes skip an inflection point to better prepare for the next one.

For example, by the looks of the popular press you would think smartphones are dominating the mobile phone market. It is true they are a significant, rapidly growing business trend. But as of 2011 there were approximately 5.9 billion mobile subscriptions worldwide[8] (87% of world population) and in 2009, 2010, and 2011 combined there was a total of 890 million smartphones sold.[9] If every one of those phones was in operation, that's just 15% of the market, leaving over 5 billion "un-smart" phones in use.

If you are in the phone business, that's plenty of customers to define a market. So, yes, you may wish to join the smartphone bandwagon. But there are plenty of other options for those who are not in the top tier of phone manufacturers. A new business model does not require immediate action on your part, and sometimes the best move to turn turbulence to your favor is to sidestep the tumultuous trend and pursue other less exciting but no less lucrative business options.

Take for example, Muve Music, a phone-based music plan that caters to people who may not own computers. Muve provides streaming music to your phone for a flat fee of $10 per month. It started in January 2011 and as of August 2012 it had 600,000 subscribers and is poised for another growth spurt. Muve is seen as a way to build a customer base in what has been an industry blind spot.[10] Muve is an excellent example of building a new business model to serve a segment of the population that has not adopted a prevailing trend.

Do not confuse this tactic of serving traditionalists with ignoring the imperative of innovation. You are buying time — not a get-out-of-innovation-free pass. No business survives by avoiding innovation as a long-term strategy.

Mastering the maneuver of turning turmoil to advantage is a key move when it comes to exploiting change. It helps you prepare yourself for the four forces of disruption: customers facing their own challenges, industries upending, fierce competition, and new business models emerging. As you become savvy in all four you will find your operations moving to a higher level of performance. Combined they capture a field in motion. Your expertise in responding will make you an adept in that churning, dynamic world.

As an adept, you will soon be changing your frustration to enthusiasm and turning the interruptions into advancement. Instead of worrying where you'll be blindsided next, you'll look eagerly for shifts in the market you can harness. Everything that before was a headache now becomes new developments with potential to explore. Where there was doubt, there is hope. Where there was bad news, there may be the opportunity to innovate. You will have moved to the frontier with skill and expertise, where great opportunities reside.

WILLIAM D. EGGERS OF DELOITTE'S PUBLIC LEADERSHIP INSTITUTE ON DISRUPTION AND GOVERNMENT

Expert Input

Deloitte's Public Leadership Institute conducts research covering homeland security, e-government, cost reduction, economic development, transportation, government reform, networked government, public-private partnerships, and a wealth of other related issues.

William D. Eggers is Deloitte's global director of public-sector research and executive director of the Public Leadership Institute. He is also the author of Government 2.0 and coauthor of The Public Innovator's Playbook, Governing by Network *and* If We Can Put a Man on the Moon: Getting Big Things Done in Government. *His experience in leadership and research gives him insight into how the forces of disruption, most notably industries upending and new business models emerging, are affecting the role of government.*

Trust in government is at an all time low. In many western countries the congressional approval rating is just about in the single digits at 10%. We have seen operational and political dysfunction in recent years. This has led to Occupy Wall Street and the Tea Party. People have lost confidence in government and big institutions all over the world.

We have this feeling that we cannot address these things, yet citizen demands are increasing because people see what can happen in the private sector. So there is this increasing gap between what citizens want and what the government seems able to do. To top it off we are in an age of austerity.

Despite all this I am optimistic about our future because it is the creative capacity of nonprofits, businesses, social enterprises, and citizens themselves — not government budgets or operations — that now determines the full reach of public services and problem solving. Government may seem stuck, but there are a lot of other players stepping into the void.

You know today NASA could not put a man on the moon. They don't have the budget or the programs to support it. It's easy to look at that and say, "What a sad time." But NASA has pivoted very dramatically. They are now saying, "This is not about NASA. It's not important whether *NASA* can go to the moon or Mars. What's important is that we *can*."

Space exploration is evolving from a venture dominated by massive government programs to one that is more collaborative. A variety of diverse, entrepreneurial companies have stepped in. NASA is supporting that. From Richard Branson's Virgin Galactic to Elon Musk's SpaceX, if you add up the resources, it is more than NASA can do alone.

You can go through every area — transportation, development, education, space — and you see these ecosystems of new more innovative entrepreneurial companies developing radical new business models to address our biggest challenges.

Many of the new entrants into the marketplace of societal problem solving did not exist 10 years ago. We have funders like the Acumen Fund, the Bill & Melinda Gates Foundation, Big Society Capital. You have conveners like GLEN European initiative. You have social enterprises like Kiva, Ushahidi. And you even have companies like Unilever, Procter & Gamble, Coca-Cola, Bosch, and others filling the gap between rising citizen expectations and government capabilities. The value is well over a trillion dollars from the initial work that we have done.

We've long had these types of entities. What is different today is the sheer size of the contributions. American companies and foundations contributed more to development aid last year than government. They are not just contributing dollars. They are out there convening people and solving problems on the ground whether it is the Gates Foundation around malaria or Kiva's one-to-one microfinance matches. This is an exciting world.

Government as innovator, exploiting forces of disruption? That's not how we typically think — but Eggers makes a compelling case that by changing our expectation of how government works — reframing it as a force for capitalizing on new partnerships and emerging tools — we can again begin to trust our federal government to produce innovation.

The Opportunity Window

When a disruption first occurs for your customers, there is a short window of opportunity for you to be of service before they find other solutions. This window opens every time your customers are dissatisfied. When they are disgruntled, they want badly for things to be better and this desire is a force you can harness. That is why I call this time span the Opportunity Window. During this window of time new value is in the foreground for those who are looking for it. But most are not looking

FIGURE 5.1 Opportunity Window

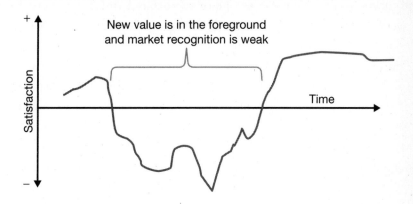

for it. In other words, market recognition of this value is weak. Thus, it represents an Opportunity Window for the savvy. See Figure 5.1.

Here is a story to illustrate how a client of mine, the CEO of a Florida realtors association, took advantage of an Opportunity Window when her customers were in dire straits and she was in jeopardy of losing her business as a result of their predicament.

When the 2008–2009 housing bubble popped, her locale was among the worst hit. In a very short time all of her members were without work, any work. Her association's services and products were no longer needed and sales quickly dropped to nothing.

With careful reflection and the capacity to see beyond gloom and doom, she identified two opportunities. She needed to get her members income fast, so first she set up seminars that taught techniques that would allow her sales people to quickly generate income with little investment.

The specific techniques she taught showed how people with the skills her members had could start and run home-based retail businesses outside the real estate industry. This move might seem counter-intuitive, but she was focused on serving those individuals. Real estate was not yet an option for them, and many of her members had survival at stake. They came to those seminars in droves.

Second, she decided to become an expert on selling houses *short*. This is the term used when a home sells for less than what is owed to the bank. When a homeowner falls behind on mortgage payments and is unable to pay what is owed, he or she is faced with foreclosure. To avoid losing the home to the bank, they go to their lender and ask for consent to sell the house for less than the amount due. If the lender approves, the house is listed and sold short.

Even though it benefits both the lender (who would rather have money than a house to maintain) and the seller (who shows diligence and receives less credit damage than a foreclosure would cause), it is still looked upon with distaste, a last resort. However, in the days of the real estate collapse, short selling was the only option for many owners.

My client studied the short sales process and, in spite of the disapproval of her colleagues running real estate associations in other parts of the country, she began offering classes. People came from across the nation to attend.

Both of these strategies took advantage of change in an innovative way. The CEO read the environment and provided value her members could easily identify. As a result she not only survived hard times but also built a credible reputation in her target market.

As people express their disgruntlement, vexation, annoyance, anger, and irritation, you will begin to hear opportunity knocking. The first step is to understand the root of the disapprobation. Trace it to its causes. Talk to people. Investigate. Make hypotheses and test them. By mining this problem you can gather the intelligence you need to innovate and at the same time use the discontent to fuel the adoption of your new ideas.

As you systematically explore and identify the causes of discontent, the outlines of solutions will begin to appear. They may even pop out fully formed like Athena from Zeus's head! Tracking the reason for displeasure and resentment will ultimately lead you to both cause and conditions, which you can address when you craft your solutions. Once solutions are ready to deploy, you can utilize the irritation and bother as energy to move your customers to choose your new offerings. Dissatisfaction is a leading indicator of innovation uptake. You just need to figure out how to generate the value that is wanted and deliver it to market effectively.

To use the Opportunity Window successfully, be on the lookout for anything that drops satisfaction into the negative. As soon as that happens, take a good look at your customers' needs. Put yourself in their shoes. When people begin to suffer, the time is ripe to act. When satisfaction reaches a low enough level that it either (a) inspires action or (b) can be used to inspire action, you have the environment you need to get traction and support for your innovations. In other words, people are ready to buy. Good strategists are *constantly* watching for these drops. They signal propitious circumstances for innovation.

Build Flexibility and Responsiveness

Being able to change direction adroitly and quickly is required to take advantage of the Opportunity Window. It is often necessary to act fast, with punch and purpose. If a particular segment of the market experiences a significant drop into unhappiness, the first provider to serve their needs successfully and effectively often owns the market. That is why it is essential that you become both flexible and responsive.

The capacity to move fast with powerfully positive impact is not natural for many of today's organizations. Unless you're a small shop, there is much to coordinate. Sometimes systems make it challenging to be responsive. It's one thing to have a consistently excellent customer service response during normal market conditions. It's another to detect a market shift, build and test an appropriate and profitable response, and get it to where it can make an impact *in time* to make a difference.

So competitive advantage is formed via flexibility; that is, versatility and adaptability. When you are not locked into a particular way of doing things and can adjust your services and products to meet opportunity, you have a definite upper hand that can be brought into play when it counts.

The same is true for responsiveness—the ability to react quickly and appropriately to create customer delight. Customers will pay for the knowledge that you will do the right thing and do it fast. Combine this with flexibility and you have an edge you can take to the bank.

Five techniques can increase your capacity for fast, effective responses to market changes of all kinds, including adversity:

1. Build a customer-value mind-set
2. Scan for trouble brewing—be ready
3. Simulate rapid response scenarios
4. Read and share success stories
5. Make responsiveness a leadership competency

Each of these techniques work to create greater flexibility and responsiveness; and each is more effective when deployed with the others.

Build a Customer-Value Mind-set

When we think of building the capacity to respond quickly to changes in the market, we are talking about creating a new way of operating. This is a cultural effort that involves creating and maintaining a particular mind-set, one built around the principle that an organization exists to generate value in the marketplace.

Organizations create that value by being sensitive and responsive to their most important constituents' needs, and proactive in addressing them. There needs to be a deliberate cultivation of this mind-set inside your organization.

Encourage staff members to embrace customer-centric ways of looking at the value you provide, including those that are difficult to understand. Do this through regular reviews of customers' needs, market conditions, new circumstances, and proactive deliberation.

Activities that support this include

- Convene the senior leadership team, vice presidents, departments, divisions, managers, front-line staff, and even all-staff gatherings to discuss what it means to organize around the customers' benefit. Bring customers to the meeting and have them validate or repudiate staff members' ideas.

- Review day-to-day operations with an eye to improvements that directly result in increased customer satisfaction, delivering more value at lower cost, increasing value at the same cost, or providing options that increase value in exchange for increases in cost.
- Institute the sharing of *best practices*; that is, practices that systematically and reliably deliver value to the customer while generating profitable revenue, customer delight, or both.

Each of these activities can be used to improve your ability to respond quickly to market changes and thus take advantage of Opportunity Windows.

The purpose of building a customer-value mind-set is to improve your ability to shift gears toward greater value and be ready to jump when the time is right.

Scan for Trouble Brewing — Be Ready

Recall the message of Chapter Three—that intelligence is essential to innovation. Do you have an intelligence program in place—a customized approach for scanning the environment to identify trends you are in a position to capitalize upon, one that is specific to your clients, your industry, your region, your assets?

Your intelligence program will provide you with advance notice of possible disruptions by ensuring that news travels unhampered to where it can make the most difference in the shortest time. Set up systems that will keep you in the loop, nimble, and prepared to succeed. Be ready before the crisis hits.

Simulate Rapid Response Scenarios

I worked for a CEO in the health care industry who liked to take his senior management team on retreat. Away from the office, he would instruct them to handle a crisis scenario as if it were real. The particular scenario he told me about was this: Congress had just passed a major new law that negated the vast majority of their services and left their customers, specialist doctors, in the lurch. They had 24 hours to design a response.

The role-playing was intense. Staff members worked through the night. The scenario stretched them in ways they had not been stretched before as leaders and team players. As they were debriefing at the conclusion, the CEO asked what they had learned. Universally, they expressed feeing more ready as a team to handle a major disruption.

Through role-playing you can seed ideas and prepare for particularly likely circumstances. I was a lead consultant on a $20 million change initiative for Royal Dutch Shell in the mid-2000s. Shell was famous for its decades-long use of scenario planning and many of the people I worked with at the time had confidence in this type of strategic exercise.

In the 1970s Shell embarked on an exercise to prepare for a variety of possible factors that could disrupt their business. With so many managers around the world, the enterprise found it difficult to respond to changing global circumstances with a single, coherent approach. They needed to be able to quickly present a unified front in the face of any emerging challenge.

They decided to tackle this problem by identifying several possible trends. This was a serious exercise and required several iterations before they landed on the scenarios they wished to use. They chose these four: the rise of alternative fuels, catastrophic accidents, political upheaval, and increases in the price of oil without corresponding increases in supply.

Shell simulated three situations with their managers. In one the shock takes place prior to the cyclical downturn in production; in another it happens simultaneously; and in the third, after. This method proved immensely effective. It was so successful that "the Anglo-Dutch oil giant was able to anticipate not just one Arab-induced oil shock during that decade, but two."[11]

What actually came to pass was a hybrid of several of the scenarios they explored. It included the 1973 sudden increase in the price of oil sparked by the rise of the Organization of Petroleum Exporting Countries (OPEC).

Although it is difficult to attribute any specific aspect of Shell's successful navigation of the OPEC Oil Crisis of 1973 to scenario planning, the fact that they had done this exercise kicked off real interest that has resulted in extensive development of the tool.

In the essay, *Three Decades of Scenario Planning in Shell*, three former Shell senior strategy managers concluded that, "Scenarios can contribute to real options at three fundamental levels. First, they can help identify future options. Second, they can help time the decision to exercise an option. And finally, scenarios can provide important input in the process of evaluating real options."[12]

By using role-playing and similar techniques that have you rehearsing for likely circumstances, you not only prepare but also create a fertile bed from which new ideas may spring.

Read and Share Success Stories

Sharing stories is one of humanity's oldest proclivities. Everyone loves a good story, especially when it is relevant and meaningful. Stories that speak to our needs and our situation are excellent tools for instigating powerful conversations. It's no accident this book is filled with stories.

When I was at the World Bank I helped run a series of think tanks on the use of story in organizational life. Participants included thought leaders from Disney, Lucent Technologies, Harvard University, Ernst and Young, the International Storytelling Center, Hewlett-Packard, Eastman Chemical, and others. We explored how story is used effectively today as part of organizational life. We discovered that stories have many uses, including the stimulation of group learning. Sharing a story among those in charge provides examples that can be analyzed and transposed appropriately to emerging challenges and opportunities. The examples help people refine and articulate their ideas. You may even wish to contact those in the stories to gather more information and assistance.

Finding, reading, and sharing stories is a powerful way to expand your knowledge, which in turn gives you more options when faced with complex choices. Knowing how others have responded and what kind of success or failure they experienced illuminates a variety of choices, making you and your team more flexible. If a story is relevant to your pursuits, it will highlight important factors and improve the quality of your responsiveness. Because stories are easy to remember they become ready references, quick to be drawn upon and applied.

In a conversation with the change master, John Kotter of Harvard Business School, we spoke at length about the power of story. He shared with me why he uses storytelling in his presentations around the world:

"Stories stick in the brain in a holistic way, better than charts, numbers, and concepts. As a result the probability that the message will have an impact on behavior goes up."[13]

My experience shows this to be true. If you want people to remember what you are saying, find a way to embed it in a story.

I have found this technique for sharing a relevant story effective:

- When you find a story that seems relevant, make a copy and circulate it to those leaders in your organization who will benefit and be in a position to take action. This criteria is very important. There are many others who might enjoy the story, but it is not doing its job as a tool for change unless it is relevant and the readers are in a position to apply what they learn.
- Include a short note that explains (a) why the story is relevant to you, (b) that you will be convening a meeting to discuss its implications, and (c) a direct request that the recipient read the story and give it some consideration prior to the meeting. Here is an example note:

> Hi Jen,
>
> Here is a story I found on the web about how our national trade association is using mobile technology to provide education to its members. I learned a great deal about the advantages of mobile and some specific tactics I believe we could adapt to our needs. I am going to call a meeting with the senior team next week to discuss this story and what we can take from it for our effort to reach and educate doctors on the go. Please read this story prior to the meeting and be prepared to share your thoughts. Thanks!
>
> —Seth

In your preparations for the meeting, go through the story and highlight the points that you found particularly relevant, adding a note to yourself that includes two important points: exactly why this point is relevant and ideas it gave you for application to your situation. Then when you get together, offer to be the first to talk about the story. Use your highlighted notes as a way to start conversations with your group. Go through the story, hitting your most important points. After each point ask the others what they think.

Generally these sessions go one of two ways: either people break into conversation spontaneously, reacting to your insights by adding their own and applying their thoughts to your organization's growth, or they patiently wait for you to finish your list.

In the former, go with the flow. Let the conversation lead you to the appropriate topics. If there is a lull, go back to your notes to reengage. If instead others simply listen while you share your learning, complete your list and then call on them to share their insights. When everyone is done, ask, *What have we learned? What is relevant to what we need to do? What actions can we take as a result of this information?*

Using this technique, your organization will build its cultural capacity for using stories to expand knowledge and thus develop more options for response to complex choices.

Make Responsiveness a Leadership Competency

One way to ensure that your team is capable of reacting quickly and effectively to a changing environment is to intentionally develop the skills required for excellent responsiveness. Many leaders value this, even rely on it, but spend little time cultivating the skills of their senior team in this area.

Just because the people in your team are individually responsive does not mean your leadership group is responsive. Very competent people often botch responsiveness as a group.

Responsiveness can be broken down into two core competencies: response speed and positive impact.

Response Speed: You will be amazed at the kind of results you can create simply by engaging your people in exercises to improve speed.

I was once a participant in an experiment on speed at a conference I attended. The results we achieved were remarkable, and we were able to generate them in about 20 minutes.

There were over 300 participants at the conference. Our emcee took us into the lobby and had us stand in a huge arc. She asked us to send a hand-squeeze from one end of the arc to the other. That is, the person on the far left was to squeeze the hand of the person standing to their right. Everyone in the arc was to transmit the squeeze by squeezing the hand of the person to their right as soon as their left hand was squeezed.

The first time we did it, it took about five minutes for the squeeze to travel from one end of our arc to the other. There was a lot of chaos and the group attention was scattered. Our emcee pointed out that we could do much better. We did it a second time in just under a minute. We felt pretty proud. The third time we transmitted the squeeze from start to finish in about forty seconds. More than 700% improvement just with a common concerted effort!

Then our emcee told us the world record was less than two seconds!! Our response as a group was to get competitive. We became single pointed — we had a Zen mind-set. We all focused. And we did it in 15 seconds.

She reminded us, the world's record was under two seconds. How could that be? It seemed impossible. Someone stepped forward and said, "Hey, I have an idea. Let's be hyper-vigilant. Everyone wake up and focus. Don't wait for a full squeeze. At the first sign of a squeeze, create a rapid response!" OK! Everyone was on board. We did it in seven seconds.

The emcee reminded us again: world record — less than two seconds. We tried again. Total time went back up to over twenty seconds.

Spontaneously four people stepped into the middle and started talking to each other. One of them turned to the group and said, "We're going to do this thing. Are you with us?" "Yes!" came the cry.

"Then let us come up with a plan and we'll tell you what it is in a couple of minutes." Then he turned toward the others in the center and said something like, "We're going to innovate now. Who's got an idea?"

About a minute later (there was a lot of pressure for action) the four self-appointed leaders turned toward us and the same guy who spoke up originally addressed the larger group.

"OK. Here's what we're going to do. We're going to send this thing around the arc at the speed of light. Now I don't think that's possible, but it doesn't matter what I think. It matters what the clock says.

"So, here's how it's going to go. When we give the signal, everyone is going to do it at the same time. Now, I know that sounds like cheating, but it's not going to be cheating. We are going to move this pulse hand-to-hand faster than is humanly possible and we're still going to play by the rules.

"This guy over here on the end is going to wait until we give him the signal to start and as soon as he gets the signal everyone is going to do a left-right squeeze. I figure that this will count because you're all going to feel your left hand squeezed before you squeeze the person on your right."

Then he paused and looked at the emcee to see if she was going to shut him down. Everyone held their breath. She smiled and shrugged her shoulders. "Yes! We're going to do this!" And then we did it. 1.25 seconds.

We had at least tied the world record! We were elated. People jumped up and down and hugged each other, introverts and extraverts alike were united in a moment of celebration.

"Hold on!" screamed the emcee above the deafening roar, "Hold on!" The room grew quiet. We were all prepared for the worst. We thought for sure she was going to disqualify us.

Instead she said, "There is no world record. I made that up." There was stunned silence and few nervous laughs.

"Look what you can do when you all get behind something. You can do the impossible. You sent a hand squeeze across 300 people in less than two seconds just because I told you it could be done. What if I said it happened in less than one second. Would you have done that?"

Then she had us do it again, one more time, by the book, no funny stuff. Twelve seconds.

So, this is obviously not a rigorous experiment. The lesson here is the increased power of the group through concentration, creativity, powerful will, and fun. We also had an emcee who, by intentionally lying to us, led us to believe that something we thought was impossible was possible. And by hook or by crook we did something that we all thought was impossible.

The whole exercise lasted about 20 minutes. In that time 300 people got our response time down from 300 seconds to 12. That's going from an average of a little over three people per second to 25 people per second!

You can create remarkable results simply by engaging your people in exercises to improve speed. Work with your team to identify the highest value situations where response time will have impact. Then experiment in ways you can measure — our emcee had her stop watch. This is the best curriculum I know for improving response speed.

Positive Impact: It's helpful to recall that our focus in this chapter is on exploiting disruptions. We are talking here about building the leadership competency of *creating positive impact* in the face of a disruption.

If you want to build your capacity as a leader to generate great results fast, you must first identify what this means in the context of your business. What type of positive impact would be meaningful for your organization? Discussing this with your team is a valuable exercise as it will give needed direction to those who are developing and leading the execution of strategy. The conversation alone is insufficient to create positive impact, but it is a necessary step.

From my work with other clients, I know that positive impact can mean

- Getting solutions to clients before competitors
- Quickly letting go of markets that are not primary targets while directing staff time to the highest priorities
- Using data to create solutions that work better for customers
- Creating tighter relationships with key partners based on exceptional benefit

- Upholding excellence in the quality of service across the globe, regardless of local challenges
- Reaching the right customers at the right time with the right solution

Once you have identified the positive impact that is a strategic imperative for your operation, you must work together to understand what that means for today's work, and how it will change for the better in the future. One way to do this is to take the impact you have identified and use it as a lens for each of your core operations.

For example, take the last point on the list above, *Reaching the right customers at the right time with the right solution*. Pull your senior team together and as a group, review each of the core responsibilities. Your conversation might go like this:

- How can *marketing* be improved to help us reach the right customers, do it at the right time—when they are ripe for our services—with a solution that makes the most sense to them?
  - What are we already doing that supports this? How can we amplify these?
  - What are we doing that is counter to this positive impact? How can we address these crosscurrents?
- How does *information and knowledge* work to help us touch the right clients when need is most acute?
  - Does it assist with narrowing down the solutions we present so the client feels served best?
  - What capabilities do we have that are taking us in this direction today? Can they be bolstered, grown, fortified?
  - What are we doing to get in our own way? What can be done about it?
- How does *operations* move us to the right clientele at the right time and bring to market the best offering?
  - Are there exceptional wins we have had in the past? What were they and what can we learn from them?

- What practices have taken place that are worth replicating? What would it take to make them standard operating procedure?

- Do we have examples of botching this? Was it a single occurrence, or are we regularly dropping the ball? What is the best way to address this?

And so on, one core function at a time.

If you have this conversation with the entire senior team, you can create synergies that address disconnects between silos. This enhances group responsiveness. As you move through each of the core functions, you will almost certainly find people and functions that can work together to achieve impact greater than what they are producing without coordination. You are also likely to locate activity operating at cross purpose that can be resolved.

All five of the techniques discussed in this chapter work toward greater flexibility and responsiveness to market changes. When you combine them, the sum total is an organization adept at finding good options and applying them for rapid results.

Building a customer value mind-set puts your entire leadership team in the best position to create results that push the organization forward while building customer trust and loyalty. Becoming expert at scanning for developments gives you a proactive edge. Simulating rapid response scenarios builds the capacity at the strategic level to mobilize and act, seizing opportunities as they emerge. Reading and sharing success stories enhances on board knowledge, building a repertoire of shared insights and ideas drawn from others' experience. Building responsiveness as a leadership competency prepares you to act fast and seize the moment when opportunity arises. Taken together these five techniques will build your leadership muscle for turning disruption to your advantage.

Value Assessments

There is one more tool to add to your kit, a protocol for assessing opportunities for the value they present. This is a critical skill, bringing the right lens — value — to bear on new developments. By mastering my

Value Assessment process, you will help your leaders work together to determine what value, if any, turmoil can provide before dedicating resources.

Value Assessment Process

I developed this process to help leaders share what they know with their senior team, quickly targeting and assessing opportunity as it arises. This is an especially helpful tool when developments are breaking fast and decisions must be made with haste. This process helps people articulate potential and then forecast both risk and reward so decisions can be made and action taken in short order.

Without a clear system, ideas may have to go through too many steps in order to be approved. Precious response time can be lost. Therefore, it is helpful to have a well-rehearsed protocol that allows you to quickly bring to light information and engage your group's collective intelligence.

Value Assessment Protocol

1. **Opportunity identification**. A change in circumstance is identified. This means that it holds promise for new value for the organization. This could be new technology available for exploitation, a change in demographics among customers, a new demographic becoming a target audience, breaking news, or anything else that shifts the playing field.

2. **The Value Assessment meeting is called**. The senior management team assembles or an agenda item is added to an upcoming session. The point is raised in advance and people are put on alert that a Value Assessment will take place so they can prepare accordingly.

3. **Meeting participants each prepare three points**. Each participant prepares for the meeting by completing these three statements:

   a. This change in circumstance raises these important issues for our customers and our organization: _____

   b. The areas most likely to be impacted are: _____

   c. Possible opportunities include: _____

- Each of these opportunities may generate enough value in the market to justify investment in a significant innovation. At this early stage of the Value Assessment options do not need to be realistic or even seem achievable. It is too early in the process to pass judgment. There is not enough information. All possibilities should be identified and explored.

4. **The Value Assessment takes place**. The agenda goes through these four steps:

   a. The person who identified the change in circumstance speaks up and shares the change they identified and why they felt it warranted a Value Assessment.

   b. The members of the cabinet each share their three statements.

   c. There is open discussion to identify what can be done near term to take advantage of the situation and to forecast longer-term benefits that might result.

   d. A decision is called for: does this deserve further consideration? Do these circumstances warrant our continued consideration and possible action?

      - If no, it's done. The Value Assessment is over. A decision has been made to stop pursuing the change that was identified. No resources need be dedicated.
      - If yes, a *Stage 2 Value Assessment* meeting is scheduled and individuals are designated to take accountability for further developing the various ideas warranting serious consideration.

Stage 2 Value Assessment

A Stage 2 Value Assessment only takes place when the first meeting clearly identifies opportunities worthy of the group's time and consideration. These sessions can happen in the same day if the opportunity is particularly valuable and immediate. The purpose of the follow-up is to deepen the knowledge among the team and determine if significant action is required.

For example, let's say your company is about to release an application that runs on a smartphone. The app was seriously limited by the smartphone's current operating system, in particular one feature of that system. The company that makes the smartphone just announced a major upgrade to be released in 30 days, including improvements to the problematic feature. You suddenly have the option of building in new functionality and grabbing market share as a result, but you have to act fast to have your app ready when the new smartphone operating system hits the market.

Here are the five steps for a Stage 2 Value Assessment:

Stage 2 Value Assessment

1. **Meeting convenes**. Participants arrive ready to negotiate resource allocation. This means they bring their budgets and calendars and are ready to lobby, defend, and commit resources.
2. **Context and purpose are stated**. Meeting leader recaps the initial Value Assessment meeting, including:

    a. The initial idea
    b. Highlights of the discussion
    c. Why it was determined that a Stage 2 Value Assessment was required
    d. Who was designated to take accountability for further developing the ideas warranting serious consideration

3. **Presentations are made**. Each person designated to further develop an idea makes a presentation that is no more than 10–15 minutes long. The presentations include both narrative and supporting data. The narrative tells the story of what they investigated, why, what they hoped to learn, what they were able to gather, and the conclusions they have drawn. Supporting data is shared. The presentations are short and to the point with additional time for clarifying questions from the others. All the presentations are made prior to opening the floor to discussion.
4. **Open discussion and option identification**. Debate and discussion take place with the express purpose of identifying value to be harvested. At the conclusion of the discussion, options are identified.

5. **A decisions is made for each option: pursue or not**. The decision process depends upon the organization and the option under discussion. The final decisions are generally made in one of three ways: by the leader, by the leader with input from the team, or by a majority vote. With a decision to go forward the following questions are answered:

   a. What is the objective?

   b. What are the next steps?

   c. Who is responsible for each?

   d. What resources are required for success?

   e. How will progress be evaluated?

These two processes, the Value Assessment and the Stage 2 Value Assessment, provide a format that can be used when opportunity intrudes and it feels like there is too little time to react. Often there is an excitement in the air—sometimes it is hard to think straight. Before redirecting costly resources or making decisions that result in a significant strategic shift, these processes provide ad hoc due diligence to ensure that you are not going off on a wild jag but in fact have located real value that is germane to the organization's best interest.

This protocol assures that you bring the right set of eyes to examining your circumstances. You need to explicitly assess value to ensure conditions warrant your attention and follow-up action. Once you have executed the protocol, you can rest assured that your leaders have worked together to determine how to take the best possible advantage of new developments, especially amidst tumult.

Understand Disruption to Exploit It

You can count on a certain amount of turmoil, disruption, interruption, and drama in business today. It's a fact of life. The disturbances ebb and flow, sometimes bringing mild inconvenience and small course corrections, but other times mounting into game changes that require speed and perceptive response.

The leaders who are skillful at managing these challenging forces are more than one step ahead of their competition. They are perpetually reacting and rechanneling resources in the face of new developments and using those developments to their advantage. That is why understanding the four forces of disruption, learning to turn them to your advantage, keeping an eye out for Opportunity Windows, building flexibility and responsiveness, and knowing how to assess potential value on the fly add up to a competitive edge.

Success Rules

- Use the four forces of disruption — customer challenges, industry change, fierce competition, and new business models — to turn turmoil to your advantage.
- When a disruption first occurs, there is a brief window of opportunity for you to innovate new value for customers before your competitors innovate a response.
- Exploiting disruption requires flexibility and responsiveness, which you can achieve by applying these five tactics:
  1. Build a customer-value mind-set
  2. Scan for trouble brewing — be ready
  3. Simulate rapid response scenarios
  4. Read and share success stories
  5. Make responsiveness a leadership competency
- Apply my four-step Value Assessment meeting protocol to target and assess emerging opportunity rapidly.
- Deploy a Stage 2 Value Assessment when the Value Assessment meeting has clearly identified opportunities worthy of consideration.

6

Generate Value

Value is at the center of *everything*. It has been at the basis of commerce since we first went beyond producing goods for our own use and began to use them for trade. Value is what we want, what compels us to pay or barter. Value is what drives all the activity tallied daily in the world's markets.

Value is not just money. Money is only one form of value. For example, there is the value of a brand. If you have ever stopped at a gas station while on the road and found yourself on your knees in front of the beverage refrigerator searching for a Coca-Cola or Pepsi among a plethora of no-name sodas, then you have experienced the value of a brand.

Investors spend money to make money. But people spend money on lots of other things: love, happiness, taste sensation, brand reputation, quality, and the list goes on. Value isn't fixed or tangible. Rather it is a *perceived benefit*. In other words, value is subjective.

This is a key point. We tend to think of value as something objective, outside ourselves, but it is not. Value is in the mind of the beholder and savvy innovators work very hard to understand exactly what that means to their customers so they can generate and provide it. That's what this chapter is about.

When you innovate you are seeking to generate some new form of value buyers find so compelling they will choose to spend their resources to obtain it. They will give you something you value in return for what they value. These are the two sides of every value transaction.

You the provider must deem what the buyer spends to be worthy of trade; that is, you must want what the buyer offers in return for your product or service. Otherwise it is no deal for you. The buyer can spend money, time, energy, political capital, social capital, or whatever else you want and will accept in exchange.

This idea of value as a *perceived* benefit is crucial. The judgment of value takes place in the mind of the buyer, nowhere else. People will pay for all kinds of things they want, and pay dearly. To tap that willingness to pay, you must do a good job of providing what they want, which means you must know your customers well.

People will pay lots of money to attend a concert where they will hear someone who is famous yet cannot sing. They will also walk right past a musical prodigy they do not recognize, never acknowledging the talent in their presence.[1] My point is again that value is *not* objective; it is a subjective call and need not correlate to an objective measure. Brands can elevate price even when there is no corresponding elevation in quality. People pay handsomely for things they want but do not need . . . all the time.

The opposite is also true. Even if it is absolutely clear to you that your new product or service will improve your client's situation, until they understand and value that, there will be no sale. They must be clear about how and why it is worth paying for and, further, feel compelled to obtain it.

Every business leader is looking for a Value Well, a plentiful source that can be drawn upon continuously to generate value. A Value Well, like a literal well containing water or oil, contains an extensive source of something treasured. In the case of a Value Well, that treasure is customer value. A Value Well can be drawn from again and again to develop new products and services just as you can continuously mine an oil well for an extended period.

An example of a Value Well is the world's thirst for design-driven, customer-friendly computers and software that work well together. People clearly want this and will pay more for it. This has been one of the Value Wells that Apple draws from. So far, they have stuck to this formula, and people keep buying what they have to offer.

Another example, less well known, is the invention of xerography by Chester Carlson, which enabled crisp, permanent copies of paper documents to be made easily. The first office copier was introduced in 1959. Fortune magazine would later hail it as, "the most successful product ever marketed in America." As recently as 2004 most documents handled in the American office were produced xerographically,[2] thus demonstrating a Value Well that ran strong for 45 years!

Both of these examples were introduced into commerce, creating positive inflection points driven by their respective creators. Neither was easy to do at first. Yet they both generated dramatic and decisive favor in the marketplace that yielded years of profits.

So a Value Well is an ongoing source of value, enabling a steady draw of multiple products or services over an extended period of time, built around a thirst in the marketplace for what that particular fount has to offer.

Lets look at how you can identify, prepare for, and operate a Value Well.

1. **Conduct research**. Let's say you have conducted a Value Assessment as described in the previous chapter. During the final steps of Stage 2, you determine the most likely places and ways for you to locate and develop an ongoing source of value. When you have identified a possible Value Well, you research it further and find reason to believe there would be a strong, continuous demand for what you have discovered.

2. **Create a business plan**. Once you have an idea of what can be done to open up a new Value Well, you have to determine if you have a worthy business case for the effort. If you've completed your Value Assessments, you should find it fairly easy to prepare a back-of-the-napkin sketch. Now it is time to prepare a formal document suitable to present to your board for approval, a business plan that includes financial analysis, especially if doing a trial run has significant costs associated with it.

Your business plan should tell the story of the innovation, including the core idea, rationale, fit with your operation and market, success factors, success metrics, market analysis, operating strategy, and business objectives. See Appendix B: High-Level Outline of a Typical Business Plan.

Your financial model should include projected revenues and associated costs over a time span that demonstrates the viability of your effort. Expenses should include trial development and delivery, marketing, fulfillment, support, and all other costs associated with success. For an example, see Appendix C: Simplified Business Plan Financial Model.

3. **Conduct trials**. This includes experiments with consumers to see if the value you imagine is compelling enough to your clients to warrant real development. These can range from focus groups to simulations to prototypes rolled out in test markets.

4. **Prepare for operations and production**. Now it is time for you to set up shop, putting everything in place to get up and running. To do this well, many advance considerations are required, including expected transactions, specialized equipment, and synergies with other active offerings.

5. **Go to market**. You deliver your products or services to commerce, often with a ramping-up period so adjustments can be made to create stability before you hit full swing. Protocols are executed according to plan and carefully monitored so they can be tuned to adapt to changing conditions.

6. **Hone your business, optimizing performance**. Real-time learning is incorporated and value generation starts in earnest. You adapt to new opportunities and challenges as they arise. Lessons are learned and kinks are ironed out as you steer into peak production.

7. **The Value Well is exhausted; activity winds down**. When output from this Value Well drops due to changes in circumstance, commoditization, competition, or a saturated market, you switch gears. There is ongoing evaluation to determine when the costs exceed the value returned. As this happens activity is shifted to a new Value Well and the waning operations are sold or closed down.

A Value Well is a source that can be drawn upon to provide a constant supply in the market. I find it helpful to use the seven steps above as a way to think about what is involved.

A prolific Value Well, like xerography, just keeps on giving and giving. Over the last 45 years hundreds of machines that use xerography have been successfully introduced in the marketplace. At the time of this writing one of the most advanced machines is the Xerox iGen 150. It is a digital printing system that operates xerographically with a recommended average volume of 200,000 — 3,750,000 pages per month.[3]

As you consider new opportunities using some of the techniques described in this chapter, come back to these seven steps. Review them to ensure that you are considering and properly preparing for all the activities that will go into making your new offering a success.

The Innovation Profit Cycle

As you can see, finding and exploiting a Value Well requires significant resources from the early stages through the end. You must develop ideas, test them, and set up operations before you begin to generate revenue. There are also costs in closing things down. I use a graphic illustration of these costs with my clients to help them take into consideration and plan for the realities of innovation.

Innovation requires often costly resources and does not return them until a significant investment has been made. See Figure 6.1 for a visual representation of profit across time.

The activities associated with idea management begin the investment. People dedicate their time to introducing ideas and developing

FIGURE 6.1 Innovation Profit Cycle

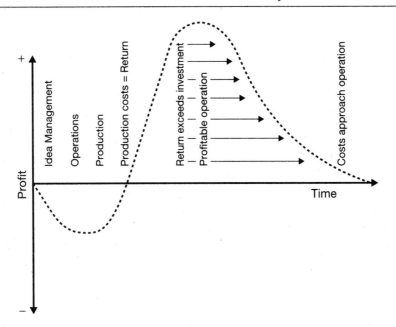

them. Costs include their time, maintenance of the idea management process, and analysis as maturing ideas evolve.

After ideas have been evaluated, tested, and selected for implementation, the costs that come with setting up operations draw more funds. This is followed by production, when the idea is introduced into the market. In the early stages of production, sunk costs have still not been recouped.

It's an important moment when an innovation's return equals its production costs. From Figure 6.1 you can see the dotted line swing from the negative to the positive at this point. It is almost as if it is a moment in time, crossing the line with a tick of the clock. While it is true that you have now justified your sunk investments, you need to take a look at the slope or steepness of the upswing to get an idea of how fast your profits will accrue. If the slope is shallow, they will come in more slowly than if it is steep.

To make this image more precise and fit it to your circumstances, an extensive business intelligence effort must be conducted, as covered in Chapter Three. For example, to get an idea of how high profitable growth will go and how long it will last you must forecast. This forecast should include factors like competition, trends, and synergies with other offerings.

Nonetheless, as a generic representation the innovation profit cycle portrays a reasonable expectation of how successful innovations perform and the overarching swing of profit, from negative to positive, that must be taken into consideration.

Your return is a legitimate facet of the value proposition. For value to be valid it must be *multifaceted*; that is, it must yield benefit for each stakeholder or it will not be a success. Let's take a closer look at the facets of value.

The Facets of Value

We innovate to generate profitable revenue while achieving mission impact. To do this well we are always concerned with a minimum of two parties: you and your customer. Value requires both of you because it emerges through the relationship.

Value is an *emergent property* of supplier and consumer. It cannot take place with only one or the other.

An emergent property is a unique quality that emerges when component objects are joined together. For example *cohesion* is an emergent property that results from joining hydrogen and oxygen in the two-to-one ratio known as water (H_2O). When the two elements combine to form water molecules they tend to stick together in a particular pattern. You see this when you overfill a glass and the water bulges just above the rim without spilling. This phenomenon happens as a result of this unique combination of hydrogen and oxygen. Because it is exhibited in H_2O and not when one element occurs without the other, it is considered a higher-level property.

Value emerges from the relationship of a buyer to a seller, a provider to a beneficiary, or even two partners who join together to do something neither can do alone. Value is an emergent property of the relationship.

Value has a *facet* for each stakeholder. Just as a sheet of glass has two sides and each may be different in appearance (or not), so value has a facet for each stakeholder it faces and these may be different (or not).

Here is an example. If I sell you a package of potato chips, you get the chips and I get your cash, two very different facets to the value generated. Both are required for a successful transaction.

Another example, but this time the two facets provide the same value. If my organization and yours join forces to lobby the government, we both increase our odds of being influential because together we represent a larger base. In this case the value we each receive is the same: increased influence.

Understanding the facets of value is important because each facet must be accounted for if a successful value transaction is to take place. If I gave you the potato chips but you did not pay me, you would be satisfied but I would not. This is not a successful transaction. Value must benefit every stakeholder or it is not successful.

Many times business owners become overly concerned with the value they are receiving. They look for ways to change the relationship to maximize this value, but do so to the detriment of their customer. Unless it is explicit and the customer has a choice, this is a losing proposition because it kills trust.

When we approach a decision about pursuing a particular innovation, whether or not each stakeholder receives a corresponding value will determine whether or not each chooses to go forward. Innovation that doesn't deliver value for all stakeholders is doomed to fail.

The Three Types of Added Value

I now show you the three varieties of added value you can exploit for innovation, and which you can combine to generate a wide variety of added value. Put simply they are: more, better, and new.

More Value

More value increases the worth of current, established value. You achieve this one of three ways:

1. Decrease the required customer investment and provide the same benefit
2. Keep the customer investment the same and provide a greater return
3. Decrease the required customer investment *and* provide greater return

Increases and decreases can happen either incrementally, in linear steps, or in multiples by scale.

A linear increase would mean there is a constant ratio between what you put in and what you get back.

For example, let's say that as a customer, you have an opportunity to invest in a simple opportunity where you will receive $3 for every $2 you put in. If you put in $2 you will receive $3. If you put in $20 you will receive $30. If you put in $2,000 you will receive $3,000. No matter how much you put in the ratio of return on your investment is always the same: 2:3.

An increase by scale means the more you as a customer put in, the greater the ratio of return.

I experienced this recently when buying business cards. If I paid $15 I got 500 business cards. But if I paid $30 I received 2,000 cards. And if I paid $45 I could take home 5,000 cards. As a customer, the ratio of my return on investment increased dramatically in my favor as I spent more. This is an increase by scale.

Obviously scale provides a much stronger incentive for the consumer to spend more. This can work in the provider's favor when there is little additional investment. In printing, once the provider has set up my order, there is very little extra expense to print more of my cards. So almost all the additional money I invest as a customer is profit to the printer. Thus, it's cost effective for the provider to offer me this kind of dramatic increase in the value I receive.

Better Value

Like more value, better value relies on existing current value and expands it. But instead of increasing the quantity, it increases the quality. This means it increases in impact, intensity, or application:

1. Impact is the consequence, effect, or influence of a given benefit.
2. Intensity refers to the strength, power, or potency of a benefit.
3. Application means that the same benefits can now be transferred to a wider variety of uses.

Consider this example of better value that is generated by an increase in impact. Previously when you purchased groceries from the Gargantuan Food Store you received your food for a given price. But now when you buy your groceries from Gargantuan you will also be entitled to participate in a consumer-driven web community where you can correspond with other consumers about quality and how to get the best deals on your favorite products. The impact of doing business with Gargantuan has expanded from receiving only the food you buy to include access to a community who will help you improve your shopping.

Here is an illustration of better value that results from an increase in intensity. Previously when you signed up to receive the Wow Brothers maintenance service for your apartments they guaranteed that each of their service providers would meet standards mandated by local and national policies. But today, for no additional cost, when you sign up they guarantee that their providers will also exceed the standards agreed upon by local consumer organizations regardless of locale.

And here is a case of better value that comes from increased application: Your credit card used to be good for buying products exclusively at our store. But now this same card can be used to buy products from anyone who will take a check.

I discuss the concepts of *more* and *better* value in detail later in this chapter when I introduce an analytic tool I developed called the ValueGram, which works with the concepts presented here (which I've termed the More-Better Value Framework). While *more* and *better* value share a characteristic of expanding on existing value, *new value* is a breed apart — as I now explain.

New Value

When you make available a new benefit that has not existed before, you have generated new value.

It is one of the joys of the 21st century that new value is being continually uncovered and brought to market. This stems from the unceasing breakthroughs taking place primarily due to new technology and its derivatives. If it's not the technology itself, it is what the technology made possible.

For example, the first 3D printer was invented for commercial use in 1984. It works by depositing thin layers of material using a nozzle that is very much like an ink jet printer. Each coat is quickly hardened. The machine places one layer upon the next until you have an object.

The first commercial demand for these printers came from industries that wanted to make a rapid prototype. The models were not necessarily precise, but they provided a good enough estimate of what could be done that the prototype could be developed further.

As the technology matured and the precision increased, 3D printers came to be used to create reliable, highly customized components. The next wave of market success came from the expanded capabilities provided by having a 3D printer on hand.

So, like many other new technologies, the first wave of innovation simply provides the new tool to those who have a use for it. The second wave uses the technology to create other innovations. And so it goes, one layer at a time, just like a 3D printer, until a new domain is formed.

Sources of new value include

- Never-before-exploited synergies
- New groups of services
- Emergent properties of novel combinations
- Applications of new technologies

The inspiration for many innovations comes from

- Unsatisfied yearnings — longing for a better outcome
- The desire to improve bad customer experience
- What was once a taboo is now acceptable behavior
- Changing market trends
- The coexistence of mutually exclusive possibilities or paradox
- Insight
- Natural phenomena applied to human ends
- Intentional stretching of possibility
- Trial and error

It is a human proclivity to invent, create, design, contrive, devise, develop, conceive, generate, and originate. Our hallmark as a species is our incessant tinkering and exploring. This has only increased in magnitude as our technological capabilities increase and become more widely available. Each of the items above represents a space where this tinkering is constantly taking place.

For example, as it becomes more acceptable to have a tattoo,[4] a practice once relegated to rogues and outcasts, mainstream tattoo parlors have the opportunity to be introduced. An illustration for the application of new technologies is dog collars with built-in GPS devices to locate your runaway pet.[5] Do you like to sit on tables? A table is not for sitting! Now it is. This once mutually exclusive domain is being exploited by the Tub Collection with convertible furniture that includes legless chairs that are made to be placed on top of tables.[6]

Each of these examples we can now imagine in retrospect. With this list of sources of new value and places to look for inspiration, the next innovation could be yours!

MARK KATZ OF ARENT FOX LLP ON GENERATING VALUE

The law firm, Arent Fox, founded in 1942 and now staffed with more than 350 attorneys in offices in Washington, DC, New York and

Expert Input

Los Angeles, has 31 practice groups and an emphasis on litigation, intellectual property, life sciences, and real estate and finance. As its chairman, Mark Katz has been instrumental in guiding his firm toward successful innovation. His secret? Learning to generate value through disciplined focus.

What does innovation mean to you?

There are two areas I focus on. The first is innovation for what we do on behalf of clients: cool new legal theories, new ways of putting structures together for people, assembling a new argument or a new line of thinking, or being creative in how we craft the services we deliver.

The second is the management of the business itself. There are a number of innovations we can implement that have far-reaching consequence, helping us to be more profitable, more available to our clients, better at helping them . . . in short, better at generating tangible value.

I used to think of innovation in the macro sense of a large-scale game-changing event. I have a new, more powerful way that I frame it today as a result of a comment you made in one of our conversations, Seth: small things done consistently in strategic places create major impact. I have taken that to heart and now apply it in a variety of ways I would not have previously thought important. Here are three examples.

When we brought you in to help us produce an offsite meeting for all of our partners, we were making a change in tone. Our previous offsites were mostly a time for entertainment and a reward for working hard all year. We conducted business but it was limited to a half-day session and whatever was accomplished during recreational activities.

This year we dedicated a day and a half to strategic thinking. We stimulated our partners, bringing in provocative speakers, staging interesting and stirring ideas promoted from within. We took a hard look at the future not only by bringing in a futurist but by

Expert Input

forming a forward-thinking group internally that was tasked with presenting at the offsite.

Second, when one of our partners visits another office, in order to promote the goal of getting to know each other better and keeping abreast of what is happening in real time, we notify everyone in the office they are visiting. We send out their picture, identify their practice group, and where they will be sitting. These are small acts that capture a big change.

Third, I send out an announcement every month on the coolest thing we did the month before. For example, when one of our partners, Pierre Prosper, secured the freedom of a 71-year-old Iranian-American businessman who was unlawfully imprisoned in Iran for more than two years.

As a leader, I can be overtaken with ideas that are grand and that become impossible to fulfill. What I have done is recategorize in my own mind what it means to generate value through innovation. Now, it is doable. I have taken what seemed very large and chunked it down into small actionable bites. Now it seems the sky is the limit on what we can create.

Katz's focus on both legal work that delivers better value to clients and operational efficiency has created a Value Well he and others in the firm can draw on continuously. By shifting to a mind-set of small, consistent, strategic actions, he has found an elegant framework to drive more, better, and new value. This keeps innovation alive in a firm more than seven decades old.

Value Objects and Value Drivers

Now that we have taken a look at more, better, and new value, let's turn our attention toward value that drives behavior. It's one thing to come up with a better mousetrap. It's quite another to turn it into a market success. The key has to do with generating value that customers find compelling—so compelling that they change their behavior. To do this you must first understand not just what your customers want, but what drives that desire. Value Objects are the tangible goods or services a buyer wants; Value Drivers are the underlying emotional motivations that create the desire for a tangible offering.

Since these can be confusing until you develop a sixth sense for Value Drivers, here's a test to help clarify the distinction. In these three examples, can you identify the value from the customer's point of view?

1. A customer wants a lipstick **that doesn't smear** in inclement weather.
2. A retail outlet owner wants **a low-risk relationship with a supplier** who will provide stock for its shelves and take back what doesn't sell.
3. A wholesaler wants **a steady flow of products that are in demand** by her distribution network.

Notice that in every case a single person is identified: customer, retail outlet owner, and wholesaler. Value ultimately comes down to individual human beings. Although it may be leveraged, utilized, or developed through business processes and technology, valuing is a human act. This is because value is perceived benefit and it is human beings who do the perceiving.

In the three examples above I purposely bolded text to highlight **what is wanted**. Many stop there when trying to identify value. But if you look no further, you will be left with the unsatisfying results of a shallow effort. In each case the text in bold highlights a *Value Object*. Value Objects are fickle, as you will see. It's a mistake to build an innovation effort around them.

What we do not see is the *driving desire* that motivates the person to covet a particular Value Object. This is what I call a *Value Driver*. The Value Object does not reveal the Value Driver, but it *is* a clue. What that clue says is, "In today's environment under these circumstances, a Value Driver is motivating our customer to seek this Value Object."

With some digging we can discover the Value Driver. That is real gold. Once we understand the Value Driver, we are in a position to generate many Value Objects as well as modify Value Objects to suit other circumstances and situations. Further, when you market to the Value Driver, people change their behavior just to get what you have.

Once you have discovered a Value Driver, you are very close to uncovering a Value Well, a source of value that can be tapped for great results over a significant span of time.

So let's revisit the three examples. This time I will identify the Value Driver for each and give some examples of how the associated Value Well might be tapped.

1. A customer wants a lipstick that doesn't smear in inclement weather **so she can look sharp coming in out of the rain.**

This example refers to a Type-A woman working in Mobile, Alabama, the city with the most rainfall in the USA. She is successful, driven, and her appearance is important to her. The Value Driver is **looking sharp when coming in out of the rain.** Once you know this, you can use it to develop a line of cosmetics, body and hair care products, clothing, and footwear designed to capture her segment of the market.

If you are successful with this line of products, you will be in a position to partner with other organizations that can leverage the market share you now own; for example, time management and business productivity tools for women. Cultivating this segment can become a profitable effort that will generate much more than lipstick sales. That is where you would have been stuck if the only thing you had detected was the Value Object. Lipstick sales can come and go. Successfully engaging a market segment puts you in a more secure position. This is because you have uncovered a legitimate Value Well, products and services that work well for professional women operating in a part of the world where rainfall is extreme.

2. A retail outlet owner wants a low-risk relationship with a supplier who will provide stock for its shelves and take back what doesn't sell

so he can leverage a very small amount of capital to succeed in his neighborhood. He is trying hard to **survive on a severe budget and low margin**.

In my second illustration you have a retail outlet owner who wants a low-risk relationship because he is facing the highest stakes: survival. If you determine he represents a viable market, you might develop a brand that serves retail outlet owners operating on a tiny budget with low margins.

Optimizing your customers' cash flow could become your hallmark. This would lead to offering other services that will increase your market penetration, including lines of credit, financing, special promotions that minimize investment, payroll processing, tax services, business management classes, and so on. And once again, you are in a position to partner with others who want a piece of this market, aggressive niche credit companies for example.

3. A wholesaler wants a steady flow of products that are in demand by her distribution network so she can establish herself as a viable partner. She is working hard to **build her customer base**.

The driving force behind her behavior is the need to increase the size of her base. Her success will rest on factors that include third-party testimonials, demonstrable history of success, brand, neutral-party certification, and, most important, references from within her potential customers' network of trusted advisors.

In isolation her need for a steady flow of products was only a Value Object. It looked like her problem, not ours. As a result it may not have registered as of any worth to us. However, once we dig under the Value Object and see the Value Driver in operation, we can decide to do some intelligence gathering to determine if there is a Value Well. If we decide to address her Value Driver, we may provide more than a steady flow of products. We can provide and arrange for others in our business network to give third-party testimonials. We can help her jumpstart her brand by associating with ours. Perhaps we can help her extend her marketing reach. (This is why so many distributors offer co-op marketing programs to their customers.)

If this approach works out well we can both cultivate her as a key client as well as provide these same services to other customers who fit her profile, expanding our offerings appropriately.

The key is always to look beyond the Value Object and establish the Value Driver. What is motivating your customers' behavior? Once you have discovered this you can do any combination of three things: (1) provide products and services that your customers will be motivated to consume, (2) expand into adjacent, related offerings that address the same Value Driver, and (3) transpose your successes to other groups of clients who share the Value Driver.

The best way to identify Value Drivers is to become very good at asking questions and listening. Here are seventeen questions you can use when talking to your customers that will help you get at the value driving them.

Questions to Identify Value Drivers

1. Why do you want this?
2. What will this do for you?
3. Why is this important to you right now?
4. What will work best for you?
5. Why is this trait/quality/request so important?
6. Is there anything about the current environment or your situation that makes this particularly important?
7. Do you have other needs that you would like addressed?
8. Is there any way this can be altered or improved upon, that would make this much more valuable than it is now?
9. Is anything happening tomorrow or in the future that makes this particularly important today?
10. How will this make a difference to you?

11. Can this be used to advance your position, your standing, or your esteem among your customers?

12. Will having this enable something else that you prize?

13. How can this be realized in the best possible way?

14. Is this connected to other needs?

15. Are there others I can speak to or work with to ensure your success?

16. Is there a back story?

17. What is the best possible outcome, regardless of how impossible or improbable it may seem?

Asking questions like these is the first step to understanding what drives your customers. Becoming an excellent listener is absolutely required. The following three guidelines will help you listen well when probing for Value Drivers:

1. **Do your homework**. Learn as much about your customers' circumstances as you can in advance. Be ready to ask intelligent questions that reflect deep understanding. The more educated you are about their challenges and situation, the more insight you will glean from the details and nuances of their answers.

2. **Build trust**. Be empathetic. Do your level best to understand and share their feelings and concerns. Much more will be revealed by a customer who feels he or she can speak candidly. Your first job is always to build trust, *then* get the information. If trust is bad, the information will be bad, too, and you will have no recourse. If trust is good and the information is incomplete or wrong, it will be easy to go back and correct.

3. **Inquire genuinely and deeply**. When something does not make sense, ask for clarification. If you sense you are getting close to the Value Driver, ask pertinent questions that will help you secure it. If your customers trust you, they will enjoy working together with you to articulate their genuine needs.

When you directly address the Value Driver, you will find people are willing to take the time to listen to what you have to say. And later, when you provide them with what they are most looking for, they will be ready to write a check for the services you deliver, invest in your business, and help you achieve your goals because they know you are helping them achieve theirs. This is the power of finding the Value Driver.

The ValueGram

More and *better* value are fundamentally different from *new* value. This is because, as I said previously, more value and better value expand on benefits already established whereas new value opens up virgin territory.

In this section I am going to show you a tool I developed, the ValueGram, to make it easier for my clients to generate more and better value. Afterward I will return to new value and show you how to generate value that is truly original, not built upon existing benefits.

Building upon existing value is often more difficult than it sounds. To break the process down, getting to the Value Drivers, I developed seven steps that use a visual image I call the ValueGram:

Step 1: Draw a geometric figure with the same number of sides as stakeholders.

Step 2: Write the benefits that drive each stakeholder on each side of the figure.

Step 3: Circle the Value Drivers.

Step 4: For each stakeholder, identify ways to create more value and better value using my More-Better Value Framework.

Step 5: Name the inflection point you want to pursue, identifying the game change that will shift circumstances decisively in your favor.

Step 6: Review the options you have identified in the fourth step and determine which will satisfy *your* Value Drivers while giving you the best chance at creating the positive inflection point you want.

Step 7: Conduct intelligence to determine viability of your approach before committing your resources to developing these new value offerings.

As I explain how this process works I will illustrate it with a fictitious example assembled from several of my clients.

Back story. Wow Brothers sells maintenance services to owners of residential apartment units. The value they offer is *best-of-breed service for your tenants.* This makes the investment in residential units profitable for the owners because they experience extremely low vacancy rates compared to industry norms. Wow Brothers keeps the owners' investments strong while simultaneously freeing them from maintenance worry and headaches.

Wow Brothers are in an extremely competitive environment. Over the last two years they have been doing well, climbing rapidly in the market, primarily due to the extraordinary customer experience they deliver to their clients—the owners—which leads to a steady stream of referrals.

But growth is leveling out into a plateau (illustrated in Figure 6.2). Wow Brothers wants to get back into a Vertical Climb, and they are exploring innovations that will generate this kind of inflection point. That's where the ValueGram can help.

Using the ValueGram process, Wow Brothers decides to upgrade their brand, moving from maintenance to protecting property investments. Let's take a look at how they used the ValueGram to identify both that strategy and the tactics that will help them get it done.

FIGURE 6.2 From Plateau to Vertical Climb

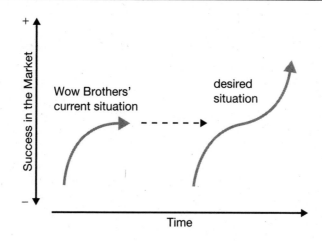

Step 1: Draw a geometric figure with the same number of sides as stakeholders. If it's just you and your customers, draw a line (two stakeholders, one on each side of the line). If you have three, draw a triangle. Four requires a square, and so on. Write the name of the stakeholders next to each side. You will always have a minimum of two, as you must include yourself and your beneficiary (your client, member, customer, and so on). In this situation there are two stakeholders: Wow Brothers and the owners. So I've drawn a figure that has two sides: a line and written the names on each side (see Figure 6.3).

FIGURE 6.3 ValueGram Step 1

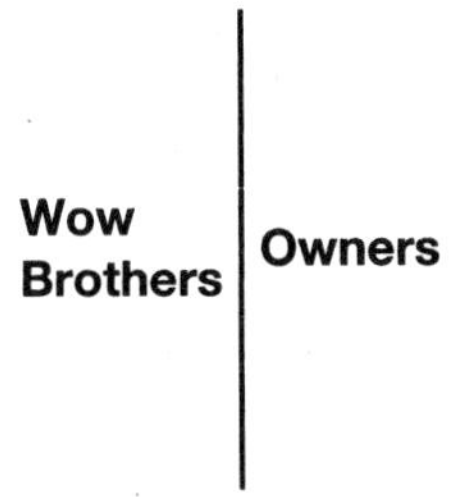

Wow Brothers | Owners

Step 2: Write the benefits that drive each stakeholder on each side of the figure (as I have done in Figure 6.4).

FIGURE 6.4 ValueGram Step 2

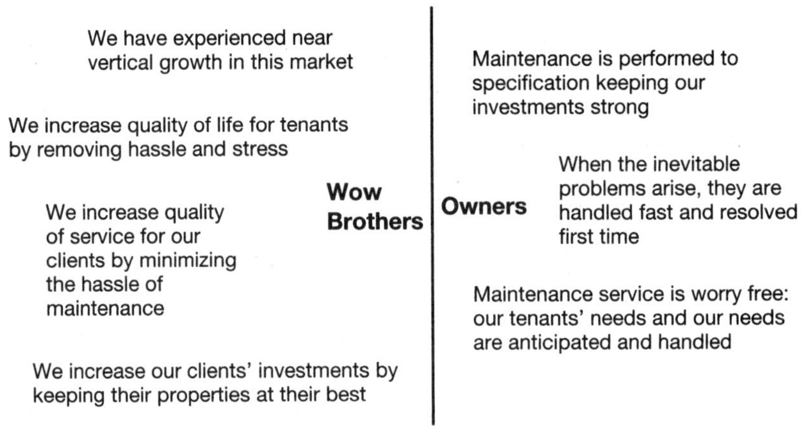

We have experienced near vertical growth in this market

We increase quality of life for tenants by removing hassle and stress

Wow Brothers

We increase quality of service for our clients by minimizing the hassle of maintenance

We increase our clients' investments by keeping their properties at their best

Maintenance is performed to specification keeping our investments strong

Owners

When the inevitable problems arise, they are handled fast and resolved first time

Maintenance service is worry free: our tenants' needs and our needs are anticipated and handled

Step 3: Circle the Value Drivers (as shown in Figure 6.5). Wow Brothers is driven by vertical growth, increasing tenants' quality of life, and increasing their clients' investments. These are the source of their motivation. The owners are driven keeping their investments strong and not worrying about maintenance.

FIGURE 6.5 ValueGram Step 3

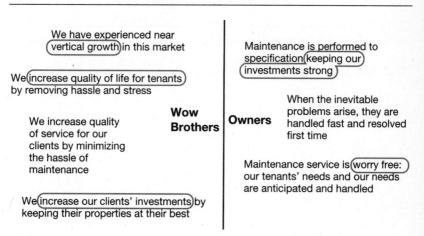

We have experienced near (vertical growth) in this market

We (increase quality of life for tenants) by removing hassle and stress

Wow Brothers

We increase quality of service for our clients by minimizing the hassle of maintenance

We (increase our clients' investments) by keeping their properties at their best

Owners

Maintenance is performed to specification (keeping our investments strong)

When the inevitable problems arise, they are handled fast and resolved first time

Maintenance service is (worry free:) our tenants' needs and our needs are anticipated and handled

Step 4: For each stakeholder, identify ways to create more value and better value. Do this systematically using my More-Better Value Framework (see Figure 6.6).

FIGURE 6.6 The More-Better Value Framework

1. Create *More* Value

   A. Decrease the required customer investment and provide the same benefit.
   B. Keep the customer investment the same and provide a greater return.
   C. Decrease the required customer investment and provide greater return.

2. Create *Better* Value

   A. Impact is the consequence, effect, or influence of a given benefit.
   B. Intensity refers to the strength, power, or potency of a benefit.
   C. Application means that the same benefits can now be transferred to a wider variety of uses.

In the accompanying sidebar I've listed the ways Wow Brothers identified to create more and better value. In this step they are not yet selecting which they will pursue, only generating a list of possibilities. This is brainstorming. Options that are far-fetched or not clearly linked to their business model are allowed, even encouraged. At this stage it is valuable to have the kernel of an idea. Exactly how to implement it so that it drives successful innovation will depend on the upcoming steps.

THE WOW BROTHERS' BRAINSTORM: IDEAS FOR CREATING MORE AND BETTER VALUE FOR CLIENTS

---

1. Create *More* Value

    A. Decrease the required customer investment and provide the same benefit:

        Provide a discount to all properties that already meet a specified high standard of maintenance. Give them a Gold Star certification. Promote the Gold Star list in publications with a target audience of rental tenants.

    B. Keep customer investment the same and provide a greater return:

        Establish an elite circle of existing clients that already meet the highest standards, achieving the greatest investment protection of their residential units. Provide each of these elite clients with certification they can display in their office and assistance using the new designation to attract more and higher-quality tenants. Collect best practices from this group, and share widely, thus spreading its impact while also spreading Wow Brothers' new brand as a provider of investment protection.

    C. Decrease the required customer investment and provide greater return:

        Create a new option for customers that bundles only the high-value services and strips away those that have significant overhead. Make this new service cheaper to buy but build in a bigger margin.

2. Create *Better* Value

   A. Increase impact by expanding or multiplying the consequence, effect, or influence of a given value:
      - Expand the *worry-free* experience while *keeping investments strong* by developing and offering a new service that (1) conducts a propertywide maintenance assessment from the investor's point of view (partner with a well-known celebrity investor to establish credibility), (2) creates an easy-to-follow guide for proactively increasing the investment value through high return-on-investment (ROI) activities that can be carried out over the course of five years.

   B. Intensify value by amplifying the strength, power, or potency of a benefit.
      - Provide a suite of new services that changes and improves the impact from *protecting* investments to *increasing* investments. One way to do this is to contact the best clients and learn their best practices for raising the value of their property prior to sale, then incorporate these into a report along with corresponding services Wow Brothers will provide to reduce costs on these important activities and make them *worry free*.

   C. Extend the application of current value by offering other services in line with the new brand:
      - Do research to find out and teach clients which purchases would add value if they were leased instead of purchased.
      - Provide leasing of this equipment that meets the ROI guidelines Wow Brothers establish in their research.

Step 5: Name the inflection point you want to pursue. Identify the game change that will shift circumstances decisively in your favor.

For example, Wow Brothers will be moving

from: Provider of worry-free *maintenance services* for owners of residential units.

to: Provider of worry-free *investment growth* for owners of residential units.

Identify the key phrases in your game-change statement. Use them to communicate with your staff and stakeholders as you introduce your innovation and the inflection point it generates to drive success (as shown in Figure 6.7). Wow Brothers has chosen a strategy of shifting from a focus on maintenance services to a focus on investment growth for their clients. Their plan is to use this to move out of a stalled Step Up inflection point and into the desired Vertical Climb.

Step 6: Review the options you have identified in the fourth step and determine which will satisfy *your* Value Drivers while giving you the best chance at creating the positive inflection point you want. To do this, combine the options you have identified or invent new ones that incorporate elements of the others.

This is a critical step. It is here that you ensure that the new strategy for the value creation you are going to pursue is aligned with what motivates you. If you do this well you will have the passion to create outstanding results.

In the example Wow Brothers Maintenance Services has these Value Drivers:

FIGURE 6.7 The Wow Brothers' Shift to a Vertical Climb

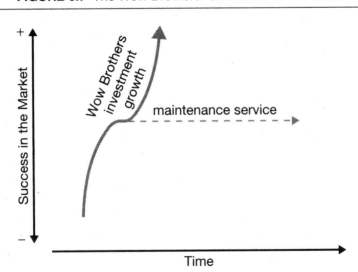

- Vertical growth
- Increased quality of life for tenants
- Increased investments for clients

To build on these, Wow Brothers developed the following plan of action. In this step they are now choosing what actions they want to pursue:

1. They will rebrand from maintenance service to a provider of investment growth for residence owners.
2. Gold Star certification will be established for the best of the best customers (rental owners) that excel in both categories: tenant satisfaction and investment growth.
3. A new three-tier set of services will be provided with the bottom rung exemplifying the majority of current clients. The top two tiers will be aimed at the double objective of tenant satisfaction and investment growth. For a grace period clients can move to any upper tier without an increase in their cost for a four-month trial.
4. Wow Brothers will partner with an investment growth celebrity. The purpose of the partnership will be to document best practices, promote them, and build intellectual property that establishes Wow Brothers and their partner as leaders in their respective fields.
5. An elite circle of clients will be built. They will receive publicity that shines favorably on them and establishes Wow Brothers as the leader in their field. Intellectual property will be developed and published by Wow Brothers.
6. A suite of new services will be developed that increases impact from *protecting* clients' investments to *increasing the value* of their investments. This will include a new service that conducts a propertywide maintenance assessment from an investor's point of view and provides an easy-to-follow guide for proactively increasing the investment value.

Step 7: Conduct intelligence to determine viability of your approach before committing your resources to developing these new value offerings. Gathering and using business intelligence was laid out in detail in Chapter Three. Next I lay out possible tactics specific to helping Wow Brothers determine the viability of their plan.

Wow Brothers can begin their intelligence effort by

- Searching the field of facility management nationally to identify investor specialists. Contact and share their idea with them in general terms to gauge reaction
- Meet face-to-face with top clients and share this strategy. Ask for a candid response.
- Interview tenants to get their points of view.
- Contact trade associations and institutional investors to get a response.
- Create a test region and do a prototype that is limited geographically.
- Hire a business intelligence agent to do a study that identifies and analyzes the key indicators for market receptivity.

These are the activities that will get them started. The ValueGram provides a step-by-step process for identifying the strategies and tactics that result in a positive inflection point when carried out successfully. Due to my More-Better Value Framework, the activities the Wow Brothers identified will be built around what they value, too, ensuring that they have the passion to carry out their new plan.

The ValueGram process focuses on the Value Drivers of your clients first and then links the results to your own Value Drivers. This way you not only generate options for increasing your value in the marketplace, but you also align it with your own business.

Most market environments are not as simple as the Wow Brothers example. Many involve multiple stakeholders. These stakeholders interact in a complex web of relationships deriving benefits that are often known only to them.

Successful innovation depends on making the value each receives explicit and compelling. Often your customer categories are in fact differentiated by the value they receive. For example, your clients may include wholesalers, retailers, and customers. In an association you may have members, business partners, and sponsors. Each of these comes to you because of different Value Drivers.

The ValueGram process works well regardless of the number of stakeholders involved. Just begin by creating a geometric figure with the same number of sides as the number of stakeholders you want to consider and follow the seven steps. Each time the ValueGram will deliver on its promise: *identifying Value Drivers that enable you to craft solutions that appeal to the others while advancing your interests.*

Creating New Value

So far I have been writing about building upon the foundation of existing value. But there is also the matter of creating new value. Creating new value is challenging because it requires everyone who touches the customer experience to cultivate a new mind-set. Simply because you are going into a new area, new skills have to be developed.

For example, if your people provide value-chain improvement and you open up a new business around choosing and installing software, the skills that are required to do this successfully in the market are significantly different and will require new talent as well as new business processes.

Talent will not be your only investment. Infrastructure must be put in place that is significantly different from the underpinnings on which your operations currently run. Unless the new value is similar to what you offer today, you can expect additional costs that exceed what is required for more or better value.

Nonetheless, new value is a legitimate and lucrative pursuit. There are leaders who build their strategy around their capacity to find and develop new Value Wells. It's time to take a closer look at some of the sources of original, genuine value that is fresh to the market.

Seven Sources of New Value

1. **Technology**. Technology has been rocking our world since the mid–20th century and the revolution is not over. There will continue to be significant changes, new advances, emerging business opportunities, and further turbulence in the marketplace. Nobody sees a conclusion to the changes taking place via computers and information technology.

   Applications are everywhere and emerging continuously. One need only look around or read popular press to see new tools, gadgets, and services breaking into the mainstream continuously.

   A recent trend is cloud computing, spawning applications that use the cloud, services that provide access to the cloud so you can use it for your own purposes, and the infrastructure necessary to maintain the cloud. These three elements hold true for any new technology: applications, access, and infrastructure. Be on the lookout for which of these can be used to deliver new value with your next innovation.

   To keep abreast of current breakthroughs in technology scan the technology section of your favorite news source. Go to media that make this their business such as *Wired Magazine* or the *Popular Mechanics* technology website. When you see a new gadget starting to make the rounds, ask the people using it if they like it, what they are using it for, and if they would recommend it to others. If you are not a technology geek, make friends with one and ask them regularly what is cool and new.

2. **Social groups**. Wherever people assemble they become *social learning systems*,[7] groups that quickly figure out what it takes to survive and then thrive, pooling their collective intelligence. The next ten years will continue to be a time of radical reinvention in the ways people assemble, interact, and create.

   Each of these communities has its own needs, desires, and unique value opportunities. Facebook is a current example of virtual communities and Facebook apps are a hotbed of innovation.

3. **Science**. Science continues to expand in three directions simultaneously: the macro, micro, and inner worlds.

   The macro is our extension into space—for example, recent discoveries of other Earth-size planets orbiting a sun-like star.[8]

   The micro frontier is the science of the very small where discoveries are increasing in number—witness the recent *nanogenerator*, an itty-bitty computer chip that is powered by body movements like snapping fingers and soon, your heartbeat.[9]

   By the inner worlds, I mean the interior of the human experience. For instance, in 2011 a paper was published documenting scientists' ability to reconstruct visual experiences from brain activity.[10]

   Every one of these represents new territory for potential Value Wells, serving the people involved and impacted. Always ask the question, how can my business make use of this information? Perhaps it is simply by *publicizing* breakthroughs in your area. For example, I have started receiving advertising emails from a business chock full of breaking news in their industry, including videos of the discoveries. They have harnessed the continuous stream of news to increase the readership of their advertising. My point is that you never know how you might apply breakthroughs in science. It could be indirect as in this advertising ploy or it might be more direct in that you may discover a new application from an unexpected field.

   One example is Minoxidil, a drug originally developed to treat high blood pressure. Due to the serendipitous discovery of an interesting side effect, hair growth, the original manufacturer, Upjohn, pursued clinical trials to establish that it could reverse male pattern baldness.[11] As a result Rogaine was invented and sold, enjoying popularity in the market. Rogaine came as a result of a scientific breakthrough in an unrelated field. Nonetheless Upjohn seized the opportunity, knowing there was a large market for hair restoration.

4. **Historic events**. History is always in the making from the latest presidential election to the most recent natural disaster. These are the changes that shape our times and often present opportunities

that can be used to our advantage. This year, 2012, a plethora of man-made landmarks have emerged:

- *The Artist* won five Academy Awards, becoming the first silent film to win since 1929.[12]
- A series of political revolutions spread across the Middle East with landmark uprisings, elections, and changes in government.
- Euro zone unemployment reached an all time high of 11.1%.[13]
- Encyclopedia Britannica announced it would no longer publish printed versions of its encyclopedia.[14]

Every one of these represents clusters of opportunity for those whose work is directly impacted.

Let me give you an example of how this might work. Let's take the September 11 tragedy and its impact on the airline travel industry. This historic event generated untold billions of dollars in new requirements that are still being developed today. These include new detection devices that meet the needs of airports and improve the traveler's experience, toiletries that are less than three ounces which will successfully pass through the security station, massive training operations to provide skills to new security personnel, uniforms for these same people, and so on.

When you see a new development in the news, ask yourself, *Am I in a position to make a substantive contribution? Are my customers' needs changing as a result of this event? Is there a service or product I am in a position to provide which is pertinent?*

5. **Mind-sets**. Our mind-sets are the way we think about the world. These models change and when they do, opportunities present themselves. The changes are caused by shifts in assumptions and commonly held beliefs, the building blocks of meaning. When the assumptions shift, new meaning arises and along with it comes advantage for the vigilant.

For example, there was a time when software was expensive, expansive, and difficult to install. As a result, most people looked for stable mainstays and did not consider switching when they found them. The mind-set was one that yearned for stability and ease of use while eschewing rapid turnover. The market was difficult to break into if you had new software that was unique, quirky, or rapidly changing.

With the advent of smartphones and the introduction of apps all that changed. Now entire market segments are made up of people who cruise apps daily looking for cool new games and programs. The mind-set has changed dramatically. People enjoy the stimulation and tolerate ongoing development and regular updates. Turnover is part of the fun. The attitude is reflected in the stance which asks, *What cool, new feature did they add this week?*

It is clear that the current generation thinks of the world in fundamentally different ways than the previous generation. That said, much has been made of the essential discrepancies between *digital natives* (those born into a world where technology use is ubiquitous) and *digital immigrants* (those born before widespread technology use).[15] There are many who have taken advantage of the new mind-sets of today's generation, opening the door to opportunity.

To the extent that worldviews can be mapped, understood, and applied, advantages will open up to operate in new space and serve new market segments.

6. **Design**. *Design* is the deliberate, intentional application of experience, expertise, wisdom, and creativity to deepen satisfaction and increase utility. Most people think of *visual* design, but other applications include user interface design like Google's elegantly simple search screen, product design like Apple's deft use of touch screens, and experience design like the Disney Company is famous for at its theme parks and events. New design opens new markets.

Design includes brand extension. For example, applying your brand to new areas of customer experience increases the reach of your brand. Consider how Ferrari has applied its brand to mobile phones, watches, and telescopes. Each of these is now associated with luxury, wealth, and high-performance racing machines.

Design covers attention to detail that creates an overall user experience consistent with a set of values. Perhaps the most famous example of this today is Apple with their uniform set of design standards that unite their computers, mobile devices, and software, including iTunes, a brand-expanding phenomenon.

Design also includes the transposition of design elements from one domain to another, such as using the design elements of computers to change the appearance of the dashboard of a car.

These all present market opportunities and regularly open up new markets for entrepreneurs. For instance, Gazelle.com began as an electronics trade-in site. It now markets aggressively to Apple owners along with several other market heavyweights. They have developed an ease-of-use online design interface that makes Apple customers feel right at home. This is an example of locating a Value Well (easy-to-use technology re-commerce) next to a thriving market, the high-end Apple products.

7. **Macro tools applied to an everyday scale**. A variety of utilities once available only to the rich and powerful have now become readily accessible to organizations of any size, including one-person operations. I call these utilities that migrated to the masses from specialized, well-financed technology companies *macro tools*.

One example of this is the massive computing power available today, as was discussed in the first chapter via the Animoto story. In that case, a small start-up avoided investing in computing power for its data-intensive video offerings by "renting" cloud computing services from Amazon.

A similar macro tool is the availability of data storage in very large amounts. There is also the advanced technology now available in inexpensive gadgets, such as facial recognition in $100 digital cameras. Each of these are macro tools that consistently yield new combinations with powerful impact.

Another macro tool that has impact on an everyday scale is mass customization: providing a unique customer experience to millions of clients. Amazon.com was one of the first examples, using customer data to display a unique set of offerings modified to suit the individual viewer. For instance, when I buy a book on ultra-light camping techniques Amazon next shows me books on hiking, wilderness first aid, and other camping methods. If *you* viewed the same book, you are likely to see a different set of recommended products, each based on your past shopping behavior.

Successfully initiating a new product or service in the market by drawing on one or more of these sources of new value may make it possible for you to secure early adopters, build advantageous relationships with partners, and secure a toehold that has the potential to create a broad base of support. All of these are the rewards of the first few innovators to bring new value to market. Each of these possible wins provides justification for seeking out and discovering new value.

As soon as a new methodology, technology, idea, product, service, or way of viewing the world gains some currency, you are in a position to take advantage of it. Every time something new crosses your path ask yourself, *How can I apply this?* Often a new development does not mature until interested parties adapt it to their own ends, sometimes using it for a purpose other than it was originally intended. So your application actually contributes to the evolution.

The Subjective Nature of Value

Tradition may tell you that value represents the worth of goods or services as determined by the market. But remember that this definition does not convey the true power of value. Value is subjective. It is a perceived benefit. If perceived value is large, the return on the exchange can be correspondingly large.

Value changes according to circumstance. The person who lays out the resources to garner the value—no one else—determines the benefit. Some customers are transparent—you know exactly what they want—and others are opaque, fickle, oblivious, or inconsistent. But it doesn't matter. Ultimately each makes their own judgment as to what they value.

It's your job to identify their Value Drivers and create offerings around it. You need to know what customers value *before* the customers do. To do this you must necessarily go outside the scope of what you consider value. Innovation is about thinking outside the box.

Success Rules

- Significant investment in idea management, operations and production is required well in advance of innovation yielding a profit.
- For an innovation's emergent value to be valid it must yield benefit for each stakeholder it faces.
- Value can be derived from delivering something more, better, or new, and these strategies can be combined to generate a wide variety of value.
- Learn to distinguish true Value Drivers by becoming very good at asking questions and listening.
- Creating a ValueGram will reveal how to build upon the foundation of existing value to provide more and better value. Creating new value is challenging because it requires a different mind-set. Every time something new crosses your path ask yourself, *How can I apply this?*

Drive Innovation Uptake

There is nothing more gratifying or necessary than seeing your offerings purchased and put to use. Uptake is customer acceptance of a new product or service. Without it innovation is an empty shell, a wasted effort. With it, new ideas come into their own as they are taken up and applied by the people who most desire them — your customers.

Uptake is critical to making best use of an inflection point. When you successfully drive acceptance, market success goes up. This is where the rubber meets the road. As your customers embrace your offering, apply it, and get results they enjoy, you are climbing up the inflection point on a growth trajectory.

In the context of innovation, uptake refers to the customer's activity of picking up your offering, making it part of their world, and putting it to good use. The best innovators help customers with these three processes, making it easy for innovation uptake to occur. They do this by creating a shared stake in success. When the customer is successful, the innovators are successful — and vice versa. This partnership gets every stakeholder working with the others to realize benefits. Working together for mutual benefit is an important shift. It changes the nature of commerce. It moves the core activity away from a transaction and toward a generative relationship.

A transaction is a simple exchange. I give you this, you give me that: we're done. It takes place in one moment of time. A generative relationship implies a longer span of time in which everyone involved works to produce new value, using each other as resources and doing more than any individual could do alone.

Generative relationships require a different kind of care than transactions. Whereas a transaction is based simply on satisfying a clear need, a generative relationship requires getting to know each other for the sake of increasing value. This is the basis of mutual development. The key is a shared stake in success.

I introduced this book with a tale of two efforts at the World Bank. One languished though it enjoyed good timing, expert professionals, and significant funding. The other prospered, grew amazingly fast, and is still around today even though it started in a back office with no budget and zero visibility. The second, more successful effort was built around engagement, pulling people in at every stage and involving them based upon a shared stake in success. Not only did this effort spread with speed, it sustained its impact and remains a viable force over a decade later because it continues to generate significant value for all involved.

Having been there I observed something wonderful and remarkable. Our customers found other uses for our products and services that we did not anticipate. For example, in the Introduction I wrote about the critical role of our Thematic Groups, professionals who gathered to share what they knew and apply their know-how to the toughest problems they were facing. Some of the people we served, members of these Thematic Groups, created their own knowledge communities that included those they were serving, the poor.

In 2012 I moderated the World Bank's conference, Mobilizing Knowledge Networks for Development. There were over 500 attendees, many sharing how they were working with networks of the poor and the remarkable results being generated. It was easy to see how this way of working extended beyond our initial efforts and had taken on a life of its own, creating benefits we never envisioned. All these are the results of uptake.

No longer is it enough to build a product or service and throw it out into the market without building strong relationships with your customers beforehand. To create the kind of relationships that withstand stress, grow stronger through adversity, and blossom into both loyalty and unanticipated value, you need to understand and successively cross four thresholds of engagement.

The Four Thresholds of Engagement

A *threshold* is a boundary that once crossed, results in a new condition. In this case there are four conditions of progressively greater *engagement*—four thresholds that must be crossed to attract and involve potential customers in ways they find compelling.

I discovered and mapped these four thresholds as part of my work in theater from 1978 to 1991. During those thirteen years I designed and produced a wide variety of experimental theater events, many in public places (street theater) and a significant number relying on audience participation.

The four thresholds are

1. Attention
2. Investigation
3. Experimentation
4. Identification

While experimental theater is a decidedly different realm than the world of business, it turns out there are some striking similarities when it comes to getting people's attention, holding it, and engaging them in your offerings.

In particular, to drive uptake you must first be noticed (Attention). Then your customers have to seek to know more about you; in other words, they must check you out (Investigation). This must lead them to try what you have to offer (Experimentation). And finally, once they have given you a shot and liked what they found, they should come to consider you as part of themselves, an essential aspect of their identity (Identification). Once this happens you truly have uptake.

For 13 years, through hundreds of performances, I learned how to capture an audience's attention and hold it when they were on their way somewhere else, as most audiences of street theater are. I began to see that the process worked best when I advanced the audience sequentially through the four thresholds.

The ultimate purpose of a good deal of my performances was to involve the audience in the co-creation of the show itself. In theater this is referred to as crossing the *fourth wall.*

The other three walls in theater are more commonly known: backstage, stage left, and stage right. The fourth wall, less often discussed, is the boundary between performance and audience. Crossing the fourth wall (that is, bringing the audience into the show) was a significant object of my focus.

It all started somewhat accidentally with my first performance, which took place on the campus of Indiana University in Bloomington while I was in school studying mathematics. Because I was new to performing I had no confidence that I could raise an audience. So I decided to try my best to grab one that had already formed.

I planned my first event to take place immediately following the outdoor performance by a well-known guitar duo. My troupe assembled and waited patiently while the two musicians performed for around 100 college kids. It was an idyllic day in Dunn Meadow, a large open park where people went to enjoy good weather, throwing footballs and Frisbees. Today they were listening to music.

As soon as the duo completed their last piece my troupe whipped into action just a few feet from the stage. We began with dancing, music, and poetry recitation. We were a sight to behold: dancers in leotards, poets in mechanics' jumpsuits, and a tall bass trombone player wearing a rubber mask of Richard Nixon.

As a producer I had an anxious moment as the audience got up to leave following the guitar performance, turned their heads in our direction, and shifted a bit not knowing what was going on. Then most of them settled back down on the grass next to their backpacks to check us out. We had successfully crossed a critical stage with our new audience: they had decided to stay.

Our performance went on for about 10 minutes and then something very interesting happened: several members of the audience got up to join the performers in the dancing. I was on the sidelines watching and observed a regular stream of people moving into our performance area.

Soon there were as many audience members in the show as there were members of my troupe.

Shortly after that when the show we had planned ended most of the remaining audience got up and everyone, including the performers, spontaneously formed a conga line snaking around Dunn Meadow. They created a chant that I can remember to this day: *I used to know somebody who used to be somebody who used to know somebody you used to be! I used to be somebody who used to know somebody who used to be somebody you used to know!*

None of this was rehearsed. None of this was in my plans. It arose spontaneously. I thought it was a marvelous quality, making the event memorable. The spirit of our art had caught and spread among the audience. After about 10 minutes of chanting in the conga line everyone collapsed on the grass, had a good laugh, and the show was over. But I was inspired in ways that influence my work to this day.

I will now show you what I learned via my experimental theater and how it applies to driving uptake for innovation.

Attention

This is about getting noticed. Because the audience is on their way somewhere else in street theater, their minds are occupied with other thoughts. They do not stand in line so they can take a seat and enjoy the show. Initially they are as far as they can be from participation.

The same is true with your customers. They have other things on their minds and being part of your next offering is not on their list. In street theater you can always grab someone's attention with a shocking act. For example, lighting a dollar bill on fire will turn some heads. But you also run the risk that passersby will take one look and flee. When you are turning someone's head you want to insert yourself in their field of attention, but do it in a way that they find interesting and not disturbing.

Direct mail has long been a popular way to try and grab customer attention. In this media the envelope has become an art form with the sole purpose of getting the reader to open it. We have all seen the envelopes that look like official documents or announcements of sweepstakes winners. These are examples of head-turning tactics.

If you are like me, you now automatically deposit sweepstakes announcements in the trash bin. This tactic is no longer interesting, but has become disturbing. It prompts a reaction that is the opposite of what the sender is hoping for. After two or three experiences with this deception I dismiss the originator as a scam artist. If I pause to open the notice or read the return address, it is only to ensure that I note the sender so I can refuse business with the dishonest party in the future. This is the equivalent of a fleeing passerby and obviously an ineffective technique for customers who fit my profile.

The point here is that you want to capture attention and get noticed in a way that will lead uninterrupted to the next threshold. If a direct mail marketer wants to capture my attention, they need to do it by honestly appealing to things I am genuinely interested in. REI does this all the time. As a wilderness camper I read almost every circular they send me. That is because I am genuinely interested in camping equipment and clothing, which they boldly display on the outside of their circulars. I have come to trust them as a welcome provider of outdoor gear.

I once ran a campaign to garner attention in a business setting. In this case our customers were employees. We needed their uptake to succeed as part of a large scale system overhaul most of them had no interest in.

I was asked to run this campaign after two previous managers had failed; they could not get anyone to pay attention. My first step was to incorporate the magnificent photography of Harold Feinstein, stunningly beautiful pictures of flowers. We harnessed the captivating nature of his art to successfully grab people's attention.

We coupled Feinstein's pictures with the tagline, "Improving the Way We Work." This was an honest articulation of what we were trying to accomplish with the system overhaul that conveyed the benefit to our customers.

This first threshold, Attention, is about breaking through the daily onslaught of information overload and irrelevant pitches and into your customers' awareness in ways they find welcome. These days our world includes more assaults on attention in a single day than our ancestors of 100 years ago experienced in a lifetime. According to J. Walker Smith, leading authority on marketplace trends and consumer buying motivations, the average consumer may be bombarded by as many as 5,000 ads each and every day.[1] All of this is to say that when a customer or beneficiary first hears of your offering they are not thinking about you. They are enmeshed in a world that does not include you. It is likely that they are harried, pressured, and working hard to keep up with other demands impinging upon their peace of mind.

Getting someone to turn his or her head in your direction and notice you is simply about registering as a point of focus. You must do something out-of-the-ordinary to grab attention. You must be interesting and alluring without being inappropriate. This first of the four thresholds is a prerequisite for the next, Investigation.

FOUR WAYS TO SUCCEED AT BEING NOTICED

1. Address your customers' pressing concerns

   Conduct intelligence in advance so you know and understand what is on the minds of the people you are trying to reach. Identify how you can help them with the pressures and problems they are facing today. Rely on establishing relevance to capture their attention.

2. Lead with the miracle

   Don't start with background or justification. Put your compelling content up front, first. Use it to grab attention.

3. Provide entertainment

   Amusement has long been used because of its attention-grabbing nature. The trick is to switch seamlessly into content without creating a bait-and-switch experience where the customer feels they have been tricked. Instead use the entertainment as segue, a natural transition into your content.

4. Tell a story

   People are story-consuming animals. We use stories to construct meaning in our lives. Everyone loves a good story. Use compelling narrative to pull customers into your world

---

Investigation

The second threshold requires you to offer something that makes your customers not only pause, but also want to learn more and check you out.

In my theater I could easily grab people's attention by simply making a loud noise. People would jolt and turn. But as soon as they realized what I had done, they would quickly walk away. They might even be resentful and feel that I had jarred and interrupted them or betrayed their trust by using a cheap trick to get their attention.

Offering music was a different story. The more beautiful, the easier it was to capture attention for more than a moment. The same held true for movement. I could jump around on the street and that would turn heads. Some people would stay and watch a bit. But most would keep on going. However, when I provided dancers, a much greater percentage of onlookers would choose to stop. Moving from something surprising and out of the ordinary to something that is not only surprising but also aesthetically appealing made all the difference.

This is what you see in advertising that attempts to appeal to the infamous WIIFM (What's In It For Me) motive. The idea is if you can quickly get across the benefit to your customers, making it appealing to them, they will stay to learn more.

What I discovered in theater was that this benefit could simply be a pleasant experience. For many people today, that in itself is worth their time and attention. People are so used to being bombarded with unpleasant advertising, they will often stop for the experience of just being entertained without a hard sell. The key to having people pay attention is to be compelling.

In the market, you are dealing with different motives, but many of the lessons from the theater are easy to transpose. To get people to choose to check you out you must appeal to their goals. The more trust you have with your customers, the farther down this path you can go in the early stages.

Once they have investigated you, it is time to show them you are worthy of being given a try. This is where it pays to know your customers and to be able to see the world through their eyes. If you have done the ValueGram exercise and identified their Value Drivers, you are in good shape.

THREE TECHNIQUES FOR GETTING CUSTOMERS TO CHECK YOU OUT

1. Present compelling reasons to dig deeper

    Once you have succeeded at securing your customers' attention, provide compelling motivation for them to peel back the covers and take a good look at what you have.

    To do this appeal to their

    - Sense of duty and professional discipline
    - Market position
    - Obligation to drive value
    - Commitment to a cause

    Each of these unabashedly courts the self interest of your target audience. This is key to increasing their level of engagement. When they detect your offering will help them with something that is already keenly established as a priority, they will be motivated to learn more.

2. Supply irresistible content

    Through your intelligence efforts, identify solutions your customers are intensely interested in pursuing. Link your work to these solutions.

This requires seeing the world through your clients' eyes, providing what they are searching for, and reaching them through their preferred media.

3. Captivate their attention

   Provide engrossing content. Choose material designed to hold their interest. This includes

   - Riveting breakthroughs in their field
   - Compelling and relevant stories of others who have faced the same challenges
   - Absorbing accounts that address critical issues your clients are facing and provide details they are hungry for.

   Caveat: do not manufacture sensationalism. If you do, this will backfire and you will alienate your customers. Instead, do your homework and find authentic breakthroughs, relevant stories, and apropos accounts. This will increase your esteem in their minds.

Experimentation

Now you want to help your customers go beyond investigation and enter into a relationship with you, give you a try. You want them to connect, to want to be a part of something special where there is the opportunity to be enriched.

To explain this, it is helpful to look at two things side by side: (a) the *Diffusion of Innovation* and (b) a technique I developed called *Priming the Gap*.

Diffusion of Innovation: In his book *Diffusion of Innovations*, Everett Rogers, the communications scholar and sociologist, character-ized five categories of adopters:[2]

1. Innovators, 2.5% of the population
2. Early adopters, 13.5%
3. Early majority, 34%
4. Late majority, 34%
5. Laggards, 16%

FIGURE 7.1 Rogers's Diffusion of Innovation Moving Forward in Time

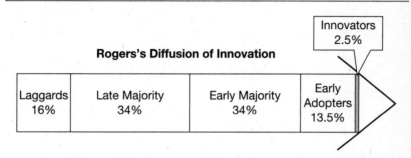

Each segment is characterized by Figure 7.1, the arrow of time showing the innovators in the lead followed by each segment in order.

Here is a brief description of the five categories using excerpts of Rogers's book:

1. Innovator—"...venturesomeness, due to a desire for the rash, the daring, and the risky."
2. Early Adopter—"...respected by his or her peers, and is the embodiment of successful, discrete use of new ideas."
3. Early Majority—"They follow with deliberate willingness in adopting innovations but seldom lead."
4. Late Majority—"...most of the uncertainty about a new idea must be removed before the late majority feel that it is safe to adopt."
5. Laggards—"Their innovation-decision process is relatively lengthy, with adoption and use lagging far behind awareness-knowledge of a new idea."

Uptake relies on the participation of the first three. The innovators at only 2.5% will jump in at early stages when risk is high just for the thrill. Early adopters at 13.5% come in as soon as a case might be made, and the early majority at 34% will follow in short order as evidence mounts. Together they are 50%, easily critical mass for successful uptake.

The late majority will come along once a good deal of the rough spots have been ironed out and it is clear that a new idea will be around for awhile.

Laggards you don't really need to worry about for our purposes, driving uptake. Although to be clear, laggards are not bad for their lack of quick uptake. It is a mistake to look upon them negatively. They are a very important segment of the market providing many benefits including stability and sustainability.

By categorizing customers in each of these five segments, you gain a solid sense of who will make the best contribution at each stage of your process. I will go through this in more detail in the section ahead, "Involving Customers."

Priming the Gap: Now I will explain my technique, Priming the Gap, and then I will bring the Diffusion of Innovation back into play for best result.

Creative tension is a core component of all art. It comes from the discrepancy between the state you are in and a desired future state. Music makes use of this when discord is resolved by harmony. This tension can be relieved one of two ways: (1) by giving up on the desired state and settling for the present discord or (2) by jumping the gap from here to there to experience the pleasant resolution. Getting potential customers to jump this gap can be a challenge. It means moving them from the relatively risk-free state of noncommittal observation to the much more invested state of participation. Priming the Gap is all about making it easy for them to jump this gap.

To prime this gap you help your customers see what is to be gained by giving the new offering a try. You do this by stepping up the benefits of the future state until it feels easier to go ahead and give things a shot than hang back. You must use benefits they know and love to do this well. This is where your work on Value Drivers once again pays off.

As the benefits become more real, valuable, and well articulated, the diffusion of innovation starts to work its magic and create the results you want to see.

First the innovators jump. They take very little provocation. They move simply because something new is available and it looks like a good thing. Once a number of innovators are involved you begin documenting and sharing their successes. This is what drives the early adopters.

The early adopter wave is much longer than the initial response provided by the innovators. As a result you have time to collect data, document successes, create presentations to share among the early majority who will begin to move once it is documented that something good is going on.

Now you have a pool of people who have jumped the gap and settled in to watch the show. In business terms they have bought their products and services. The third threshold separates the lookers from the buyers. But they have not yet gone to the extreme of identifying themselves with their purchase. That is the next and final threshold.

How to Get People to Try You Out

Customize your calls to action by appealing to the styles in each of the three groups below. A solid campaign will do all three simultaneously by providing discrete options, allowing each of these adopters to select the alternative that best fits their preferences:

1. Innovators — For these customers, broadcast benefits that appeal to people who are fearless and spunky. Lay out the rewards that may come to the biggest risk takers. Often the size of the reward increases with the size of the risk. This hampers the meek or conservative, but not the innovators! Because they like to be on the bleeding edge, you can advertise the immense returns that are possible. It need not even be likely! This group will respond to phrases like, *in extreme circumstances, against the odds,* or *limited to the first few*.

2. Early adopters — For these folks, share results that can reliably be recreated by those who are both intentional and success oriented. Anything that has been established as achievable by people who are clear, focused, purposeful, disciplined, and effective will be found attractive by this group. This gives you quite a few options, as those are the preconditions for most successes. Lay out the requirements

transparently. For example, *Through consistent, disciplined follow through and rigorous execution of the step-by-step instructions the results have been systematically achieved.* That is exactly what the early adopters are looking for.

3. Early majority — This group will react favorably if you lay out the path taken by the successful innovators and early adopters. The early majority wants to see that the way has been forged forward. Once there is a clear trail they will select it. No bushwhacking for them. But it does not take much to illustrate. Simply tell the stories of the early adopters and show the evidence. That is what the early majority needs to take action.

Identification

Identification separates those who have bought from those who will take a stand on your behalf. When people identify with your offering, seeing it as an expression of who they are, you have achieved full participation. Brand loyalty kicks in with unprecedented force. These people will do more than any other group on behalf of your success. When you make a mistake, they will pick you up broken and mangled and carry you across the finish line. Then they will nurse you back to health. Afterward they will tell you that you were magnificent. This is because they love you. It is this kind of relationship that every business leader hopes for. This is your tribe.

How to Create Identification:

1. **Target those who are already aligned**. Go to people whose identity is already aligned with your offering, not inconsistent with it. This sounds intuitive but you would be surprised at the number of offerings that go out to people whose interests are in no way aligned with them. Think, for example, of high-end luxury condos that are marketed through massive direct mail campaigns that do not take into consideration income bracket.

2. **Provide tools that aid identification**. Furnish your customers with ways to demonstrate their identification with your brand — things they genuinely find fun or useful that reinforce their connection to you.

For example, after I bought my BMW I received an invitation to test drive a BMW, Lexus, and Mercedes, on a race track with a professional driver sitting next to me. It was free. When I showed up I was given a high-quality BMW baseball cap. Not only did this experience fit with my new identity, it reinforced my allegiance to BMW because I was able to compare my car to the other brands in a domain where BMW clearly exceeded them — race car driving. This was an experience I was not likely to have otherwise.

We amateur drivers filled out a rating sheet after the racing experience. These sheets provided BMW with a source for testimonials that further deepened our identification with the BMW brand especially among those of us they chose to quote.

Did I wear my hat? Did I tell others what it was like to exceed the limits of speed in a BMW? Do I consider myself a BMW guy? You bet.

What experiences can you provide that will make your best customers identify with you? What cool things or experiences would they like to have that you can offer at little or no charge? What tools do your customers use in their day-to-day work that you could provide with a brand logo?

3. **Reinforce identity**. Find ways for clients to see themselves reflected in your brand. This is extremely effective. When they identify with you, they see you as part of their identity. Your relationship becomes reciprocal, mutually-reinforcing. Getting clients to identify with you can be as simple as including people who look like them in your advertising, having your frontline staff dress like your customers, and choosing media that are the vehicles of choice for your customers.

Another way to reinforce identity is to invite your beneficiaries to be part of your community. This does not mean receiving a newsletter that goes out to all of your customers. Bring them into your *inner* circle. Invite them to be part of important decisions. Make them feel special. When you are a member of a community you are more than a recipient, you are a co-creator of the future, a guardian of the community's survival and integrity.

There is a particular group of those who identify with your offering that you want to tap, evangelists. Evangelists provide word of mouth marketing because they believe so strongly in their experience, trying to convince others to buy and use what you offer. Provide them with all the tools they need to spread the good word. Give them your bible, your personal philosophy and code for understanding the universe. You might literally provide them with a manual for success, a book of stories that illustrate the validity and joys of their path.

When you have targeted those who have already demonstrated alignment with you and your offerings, provided tools and experiences that facilitate identification, and reinforced identity by bringing people into your inner circle, you will find that you have cultivated an extremely valuable and specialized set of clients. These are the people who will partner with you most powerfully, helping to realize the value you provide and telling others about it in compelling ways.

The four thresholds of engagement—Attention, Investigation, Experimentation, and Identification—sequentially step your customers into greater and more valuable relationship with you. They provide an easy-to-understand framework for engaging those who will become your best clients, pulling them closer to you, and preparing them to help you drive uptake.

The best efforts to drive uptake depend on creating mutually satisfying goals, built around a shared stake in success. This shared stake facilitates enlightened self-interest. This happens when people act in the interest of the groups to which they belong because they believe that in the long run it will benefit them.

Create a Shared Stake in Success

Every innovation effort I work on depends on support from a variety of fronts. Because I want my success to mean your success I always work to create a shared stake in success. That way I am working for you and you are working for me. I find the best results come that way. Innovations succeed when their importance, significance, and value are shared. This is the best way to secure customer engagement and drive uptake.

I once worked with the CEO of a transit organization in which the bus mechanics and drivers were performing poorly. His innovation was to transform the organization through personal attention rather than mandate. His organization had a long history of proclamations, dictums, and decrees all of which had proven ineffective. He designed a new approach, one which he hoped would turn around the entire agency. His framework was built upon informal, personal encounters with leadership, and through it he intended to regenerate and remake every aspect of public transportation in his region, extending the care he and his leadership team provided to his employees, their processes, and beyond to the riders and their families.

He took his case directly to the garage where he met with both drivers and mechanics informally. He explained to them how important their jobs were to the safety of the public and asked what could be getting in the way. It turned out to be a complicated circumstance involving pay ceilings and the union. There was not a resolution that he could craft without the participation of union leaders and policymakers. Nonetheless he let the mechanics and drivers know that his success depended on their success and he would do everything he could to achieve what they wanted.

He worked on that issue for over two years before a successful resolution was reached. The entire time he had the growing goodwill of the drivers and mechanics to support him because of the time he spent with them in the garage and subsequent meetings that took place off-line whenever there was a chance. They formed an unofficial partnership based on a shared stake in success. Ultimately this partnership paved the way for overcoming difficult odds, changing public policy, and resolving tricky negotiations with union organizers.

Most important, it extended to the public — the ridership who validated his work with a powerful climb in esteem and support for the transit agency. This support turned into funding when the public voted, pride of ownership by the riders as expressed through increased cleanliness and civility, and a changed image for the entire region as their exemplary reputation for public transportation was recognized nationally.

The success of the CEO's innovation was built upon uptake, first by the drivers and mechanics, then by all of operations, and finally by management as the public began to express its appreciation. By creating a shared stake for all, the CEO sparked goodwill that led to regional success typified by safe, effective transportation.

Four Techniques for Creating a Shared Stake in Success

1. Exceed expectations when it comes to serving your clients. Meet with them face-to-face. Discuss how your efforts can translate into creating a better future for them starting now.

2. Invest in intelligence with the goal of identifying mutual goals you share with your clients. Do your homework. Align your best efforts with improving your customers' situations. Let them know it and report to them your setbacks and wins.

3. Write up your understanding of what your customers need in an easy-to-read one-page summary and distribute it widely. Ask for comments and feedback. Then act quickly and decisively on what you learn. Demonstrate your intent with results that matter. Publish your results through the same channels.

4. Find ways to see the world through your customers' eyes, to understand and appreciate their perspective. Customers will see things differently from you and they will only be invested in your offerings if you give them what they value.

If you want customers to change their behavior, pick up a new product or service, get involved in your offering and take on the challenges that come with it, you must first understand and meet their needs. Then you must show them in ways that are easy to understand what value they can derive from what you have to offer.

It behooves us as leaders to make the customer a real force in the workplace. We must build the infrastructure that allows us to be open and responsive to our customers as partners in our success, listen to them because they see the world differently, and wrestle with the stress their perspectives create in our lives.

MARK HURST OF CREATIVE GOOD ON GETTING CLOSE TO CUSTOMERS

Hurst, a digital native, is author of Bit Literacy: Productivity in the Age of Information and E-mail Overload, *founder of Creative Good, and host of the annual GEL conference. Creative Good is a customer experience consulting firm that helps businesses create better experiences for their customers. Their clients include AARP, Constant Contact, Credit Suisse, Kenneth Cole, Macy's, M&M/Mars, MetLife, MGM, Microsoft, National Geographic, P&G, Victoria's Secret, and a host of others.*

Customer service and customer experience are both legitimate concerns, but they are different beasts. Customer service is the older of the two and relegated to fixers. People come to you with a problem and need it to be fixed. This is not a profit center. These people have already bought the product.

Customer experience is an invitation to see everything your customer does through the eyes of the customer. This is totally different from customer service. This is about things like

- What is the initial messaging the customer gets?
- Do they know who we are and what we offer?
- Do they get an invitation in a friendly and accessible way?
- Is it easy for people to start business with us, whether it is going to a website and conducting a transaction or walking into our store or picking up the phone and giving us a call?

Expert Input

- Do people get immediate value out of interacting with us?
- Do we have adoption triggers where people are being rewarded for getting more involved in our service and are they spaced in a way that is not overwhelming?

If you talk to executives and ask what they think of the customer experience you'll rarely hear them say, "Oh, I don't really care about that." They will not disparage the importance of customer experience. The standard line is, "Customers are number one."

But if you ask, "When was the last time you observed a customer in person using or attempting to use your product or service?" you have to be careful because you can tick off people if you ask this. Many executives never see a customer, in person, using their product or service. The closest they come to that is looking through some metrics.

There is nothing wrong with data and metrics, but it doesn't give you a sense in your bones about the customer experience you are creating. You have to spend time with customers to gain fluency around that.

So few companies take customer experience seriously that the ones that do have an enormous advantage. If you want examples of companies that do take it to heart, just look at any industry and identify the leading company. The winners today increasingly are the ones that make customer experience primary: Apple, Amazon, Zappos. Look at JetBlue, Southwest, and Virgin America as opposed to, say, United.

How many industries need to be defined by this one idea before executives begin to take it seriously? They don't teach this in B school. The people who excel didn't learn this in a classroom.

Mark's work reveals the paradigm shift possible when leaders move from "business-as-usual" customer service to a deep understanding of their customers' experience.

Involving Customers

The best way to create a shared stake in success is to involve your customers in your innovation process. When your efforts and results are fully, comprehensively, and powerfully aligned with what your customers value, they will be more than eager for your innovations. They will be yearning for them, talking to each other in anticipation, and creating new applications. That is what drives uptake, what will enable you to succeed beyond your expectations, and is why you must find ways to involve your customers in every key activity. Let's take a look at the six activities described in the previous chapters in this book to identify some helpful ways to involve customers in each.

Pursuing and Leveraging Inflection Points: Your customers are one of your key sources of information when it comes to detecting inflection points that are forming and understanding how best to take advantage of them. More than once I have interviewed my client's customers to learn directly from them powerful market forces they want my client to take advantage of.

One of my clients in particular found himself in the middle of an industry in real jeopardy and having genuine difficulty serving his customers. New technology had upended everything, making it impossible for many of his clients to operate their businesses successfully. They were tanking or being bought up by bigger players. Time and again, when talking to those who were suffering the most, they asked for very specific guidance on the future of the industry. They wanted research on new developments and case studies that told the stories of successful entrepreneurs in the current turbulent environment. They wanted classes on how to implement new technologies, and they wanted financing to buy new equipment. By getting into each of these fields my client was able to provide much needed services to his customers and transform his business at the same time. He rode an inflection point through a very difficult juncture in our economy, making a name for himself as his customers' advocate. Much of his critical guidance came from the customers themselves.

When your customers help you discern major trends and prepare to use them for market success, they are deeply engaged in your success. This arrangement allows you to drive uptake as a way to deliver the best possible outcomes to both you and them. When uptake becomes the vehicle for their success, you are positioned ideally for market success.

Building Innovation Capacity: When I refer to talent and leadership in capacity building, I am not just talking about staff members. Find customers who can be top performers in your organization as well. Not only is there great joy in serving highly talented customers, but they educate and demand more from you. Often you rise to your potential when they make demands. This builds your capacity where it clearly counts: in full-frontal engagement with the customer.

I have been engaged by over thirty executive directors of associations and I notice those who find a way to bring in and collaborate with top-notch volunteer leaders to serve on their boards and executive committees have the most powerful initiatives. These volunteers increase capability for the organization and generate more powerful results. When times are hard, they back the organization, helping it resolve challenging issues and adding bench strength to leadership. This increase in the number of skilled leaders puts you in a position to take on more, deal more effectively with critical issues, confront bigger problems, and pose grander solutions.

Greg Balestrero, former CEO of Project Management Institute (PMI), contributed to the rapid growth and globalization of his organization. In 1997 PMI had 33,000 members and credential holders worldwide, with 95% in North America. When Balestrero departed in 2009, total members and credential holders had grown to 480,000 with 13% in Europe, the Middle East, and Africa; 14% in Asia Pacific; 5% in Latin America; and the remaining 68% in North America.[3]

A key component of his effort was his relationship to member leaders. Balestrero delivered a presentation, "Global Expansion and

International Partnerships," to one of my CEO symposia in Washington, DC. There he shared the critical contribution of member leaders and how working closely with them was a key factor in PMI's success. This included the transformation of the PMI Board into a powerhouse of strategic human capital. Board members received high-level professional training in everything from strategy to media interaction. They were held accountable for the design and oversight of ambitious goals as well as relationship development. The increased capacity they brought to PMI accelerated the uptake that drove the organization to sustained growth.

Involving customers in the development of think tanks, high profile initiatives, and special projects is more than a great way to enlist their participation, it is a boost to the organization's capabilities. By making them part of your capacity development, you put yourself in the best possible position to drive uptake. They add competencies, proficiencies, and skills to the organization's firepower while simultaneously increasing touch points to the customer base through their presence. This is a powerful combination that can both speed up and increase the intensity of traction for new offerings.

Collecting Intelligence: Not only are customers a great source for intelligence, they can be some of your best intelligence gathering agents. By forming key partnerships with high-value customers you can ensure that you have access to relevant information in a timely manner. Because they live and work on your front lines, they can be the first to get news, developments, trends, and concerns. If you cultivate them as an intelligence source you can speed up the flow of this information to the points in your shop where it can have the best possible impact, from changes in tactics to adjustments in strategy. Both of these can increase the quality of your uptake resulting in faster and stronger adoption.

I have one client who runs a facilities management office for a branch of the armed forces. He makes a point of talking to key clients on a regular basis to understand their needs and how he can serve them better. He has done an excellent job of building relationships with his top customers. He does not receive favor in exchange for these relationships. The government prohibits that. But he does value these people, their expertise, and their experience.

As a result he is able to continuously improve his understanding of the changes his industry is facing, the unique needs of the people and agencies he serves, and market trends that roll toward him well before they reach him. He has a personal intelligence network supplying him with valuable information that keeps him on his toes and relevant to a changing sector and work environment. He is able to take this information into consideration and direct his staff to more tightly serve customers' needs, generating greater receptivity to his ideas and more thorough adoption of new products and services.

Making your key customers a critical component of your intelligence activity ensures that you stay in touch and are at your best when it comes to driving uptake.

Shifting Perspective: The first perspective you want to master is your customer's and it is often not easy to grasp. Clients live in a different world beset by distinct forces that push and pull them in ways we cannot appreciate unless we walk a mile in their shoes.

A great way to shift perspective is to take on the role of the client, not just in relation to your offerings, but more expansively. I recommend spending time with your clients, shadowing them, and learning what it is like to operate in their world. This will teach you why they do or don't accept what you have to offer, dramatically influencing your ability to generate uptake.

When I worked with the multi-billion dollar pension sales team I mentioned earlier which had star performers across the country, each member had a strong personality and made things happen . . . their way. My job was to raise the bar on everyone's performance by creating an event in which they would be the teachers and the students, each revealing their favorite tactics and techniques for the others' benefit.

I held interviews to listen to success stories and identify strengths in preparation for the master class. Even the most junior person was a star producer, selling hundreds of millions of dollars of product.

Without exception every person I spoke to spent quality time with customers. They went the distance. They did more than have long conversations to understand customer needs. They showed up to meet face-to-face regularly, making personal contact. They spent recreational time together and talked about family.

They wanted to understand their clients inside and out, how they made decisions, what was important to them, the world they lived in. They made it a point to ask their customers about key decisions and market conditions periodically so they could understand their clients' perceptions and how they made their choices. They actively engaged their customers, challenged them on key business decisions, learned from them. They took their education seriously.

This intense engagement with several key clients kept the top performers on their toes, tested and provoked them to learn more and think about the world differently. They were always shifting perspective, learning how their customers viewed the world. As a result they were able to create a context that made sense to their customers when it came to innovations. This context made all the difference in the world when it came to uptake. Their clients more readily took in new ideas, gave new services and products a try, and therefore fledgling innovations were more successful.

By engaging your customers to help you track their perspective, you put yourself in the best possible position to drive uptake. Learn what drives their behavior, understand the complexities they are facing, and ensure solutions are built to their needs. It can be as simple as asking what they require once you have established a foundation of mutual trust. Or it can be as complex as wrestling through a bind they are facing, taking on the challenges they confront, and putting in the time it takes to craft a solution they fully appreciate. Either way, getting close to your customers is an investment that increases your ability to create traction, connection, and acceptance.

Exploiting Disruption: Earlier I identified customers facing their own challenges as one of the four forces of disruption. I highlighted three solutions each to the three specific challenges associated with this disruption. Each of these requires you bring the customer directly into the process.

Getting tight when things are rough is a powerful way to strengthen relationships. Often when challenges emerge relationships are tested. Some people find it troubling to face difficulties and they don't reach out when trials arise, especially when solutions are not forthcoming or clear. Others get bogged down in their own demands and focus inward. Relationships suffer as a result.

If you reach out to assist in the midst of disruption, you will mostly be welcomed. Your goodwill along with any services you can provide will stand in sharp relief to the absence of others. What you learn by facing challenges together will give you a solid education on your customers' needs.

During the downturn of 2008 I had several clients that were hit particularly hard. They were leaders of multimillion dollar organizations, international in scope. Their reserves shrunk dangerously low. Operating budgets had to be slashed. They were faced with strategic decisions in a very difficult environment. I offered my consulting services *gratis* to help and was taken up on the offer.

The time I spent working on these knotty problems with these leaders was special time — it had a quality of genuine camaraderie that went beyond what I had previously experienced. By being there for them in a time of need we formed a bond that persists to this day. I got to know my customers deeply and forged connections that flourished heartily afterwards. Because of this, when it comes to introducing new products and services, there is more than receptivity, there is a shared stake and collaboration ensues.

Often with new products and services there are bumps in the road. When you have this kind of engagement, customers will work hand-in-hand to adjust the new offerings until the value is apparent.

Generating Value: Customers are in a unique and powerful position to help you generate value — they are key recipients! Any activity you include them in when it comes to generating value *is* driving uptake. Conducting any of the activities in the previous chapter *with your customers* is recommended.

One of the most powerful contributions customers can make is to help you separate Value Objects from Value Drivers. In the last chapter I talked about how the best way to identify Value Drivers is to listen and ask questions. That said, there are many ways to listen besides directly engaging your customers in discourse. Here are four other ways to "listen" to them, learning what you can about what they value:

- **Learn how they spend their time and money**. What people choose to do with their resources is a telltale indicator of what they believe is important. Get to know where they spend what they have and ask yourself, Why is this important? What does this accomplish for them?
- **Watch what your clients' colleagues and subordinates do**. Colleagues provide insight into parallel worlds. They face similar issues but sometimes craft other solutions. Subordinates respond to the needs of their bosses. Their behavior is a reflection of demands expressed by your clients.
- **Know where they are developmentally and what issues they are working on**. People behave differently at different points in their development. Start-ups have different cash flow issues than mature companies and therefore different needs.
- **Notice the kinds of questions they ask**. What people want to know about gives you insight into what they need to know. Scrutinize and follow up on customer requests. Learn what you can about why they came to you with that particular request or question and what is behind the inquiry.

Finding ways to include your customers in value generation can pay off handsomely and not just in dollars. Ultimately your goal is to provide value that your clients can count on in ways that work best for everyone involved.

When your customers deeply understand what you are able to do and in fact help you to do it, they are in the best position to spread the word, share with others how to get the most out of your offerings, and act as an uptake agent themselves.

You should be involving customers in every one of the key activities where it makes sense. I encourage you to stretch and find ways to appropriately include them. They bring a unique and necessary set of perspectives that will influence and support your goals. At the same time, they are present to see you in action, get to know your shop, build relationships with your staff, and appreciate the hard work you are doing on their behalf.

This means as you begin to roll out new products and services they are no stranger to your intents and goals. They are in a position to become early adopters and help you get the word out to the early majority, contributing directly to uptake.

Build Presence Through Value Pulses

A Value Pulse is a steady sequence of value delivered to your customers in a rhythm they come to expect and depend upon. The Value Pulse, like a heartbeat, delivers something they can put to use to fuel their interest or growth. As a result your customers will grow accustomed to your support and presence.

For example, every month like clockwork you release an industry report that contains information such as market trends that impact your customers, developments among their competitors, and keys that indicate how their customers are likely to behave. The regularity combined with quality content enables your customers to depend on it and use it to make strategic decisions, identify new markets, target current offerings, and so on. Establishing a rhythm creates expectation, a form of familiarity that weaves you into the fabric of your clients' business.

Through Value Pulses you become a regular part of your client's world and known for what you provide that they want or need. This increases the trust and rapport they experience with you and puts you in a position to open up conversations about new products and services. In this way Value Pulses create a systematic and timely connection to your customers which you can build upon to gain acceptance, trials, and even application of your new products and services. As a result Value Pulses open the door to greater uptake.

The Value Pulse is methodical and orderly. Each pulse in the rhythm reinforces the others, making it part of a larger effort. Each pulse is like a note in a song, acting not in isolation but in constellation, working with the notes that come before and after to form a composition. In this case the Value Pulses together compose greater engagement, deeper relationships, and the value potential that springs from them.

For a Value Pulse to be effective, it must steadily and consistently provide customers with something they can use to improve their situation, something that is uniquely associated with you. So, using the example of the industry report mentioned earlier, it cannot be simply a compilation of data. Instead the data must be interpreted by you, the story told as only you can tell it. And it should carry your brand. You might call it the [Your Name] Monthly Market Report.

At the same time it must also move your goals forward. Let's say, for example, your goal is to sell intelligence services. Then the [Your Name] Monthly Market Report should be targeted to your customers, display your unique acumen, and establish you as a player in your customer's eyes. Whatever your goals, the Value Pulse becomes a way to make regular, sustained progress by periodically reestablishing your ability to make a substantial contribution to your clients condition.

I once worked for a professional services firm that was holding a series of working sessions with key clients over the course of a year. The sessions took place bimonthly and were designed to identify areas of mutual interest that could be exploited with each side receiving more than it cost them to participate. The goal of the services firm was to grow business with key clients. This was broken down into three stages:

- Stage 1 was scheduling and holding these working sessions. Traction was measured by the number of confirmed sessions that turned into productive explorations for new value. Stage 1 began immediately and continued at regular intervals into the future.

- Stage 2 was the number of resulting conversations that took place with potential new customers inside the key client organizations. Stage 2 was expected to begin within 60 days following a working session.
- Stage 3 was actual contracts that resulted in profitable revenue. Eighteen months was set aside for Stage 3 to begin. The thinking was that Stages 1 and 2 would eventually result in contractual work.

These joint sessions were an example of driving uptake through a bimonthly Value Pulse. The rhythm established opportunities for the service firm to introduce new products and services, get valuable feedback on developing their fledgling innovations, and even find customers who were willing to be innovators and early adopters alongside the firm, establishing significant partnerships along the way.

Value Pulses of many kinds can also help you drive uptake by progressively introducing new ideas, finding clients willing to prototype innovations, and establishing alliances that pursue value for each other, thus generating more than either could muster on their own.

Ten Ways to Create Value Pulses

1. Periodic working sessions conducted with clients to discover mutually beneficial activity; for example, building ValueGrams together
2. Customized missives that address issues your clients yearn to master; for example, special reports
3. Regular webinars designed to introduce new business to customers, helping them to grow
4. Systematic scheduled releases of new products that your customers can put to immediate use
5. Regular open seminars that introduce your key clients to other clients they may either hire or do business with
6. Periodic videos that target a specific need and build your clients' capacity

7. One-sheet overviews that you release regularly to provide your customers with market intelligence they can depend on

8. Regularly scheduled open houses that bring clients together while showcasing achievements in an open and friendly way so they can make use of them

9. Recurrent special invitation dinners to meet with celebrities in a given industry, demonstrating your ability to connect your customers to their leaders

10. Seasonal or cyclical knowledge events that link the people you serve to valuable experience and expertise

Each of these examples provides a periodic infusion of value to customers, establishing you as a contributor and opening the door for further engagement. This process connects you with the customer in a way that enables uptake to happen more effectively. Rather than starting with a cold call, you operate from a rapport built upon real contributions. When new products and services are developed, any customer who has been the recipient of a Value Pulse has a greater likelihood of acceptance as long as the offering is germane to their needs. This is how the Value Pulse builds the kind of presence that leads to greater and more efficacious uptake.

Accelerate Growth through Value Surges

Once a Value Pulse is established, the expectation of more value to come at regular intervals is in place. You can utilize this to deliver a forceful push that is likely to be received favorably, based on the trust developed through the Value Pulse. This push can generate dramatic forward movement for your customers and a swift acceleration of growth for you. This is a Value Surge.

Here is an example of a Value Surge in action. I worked for a defense contractor who was reaching out to customers by providing regular briefing sessions on new technologies and how they can be applied to challenging issues. This is an environment that is characterized by intense competition and strict secrecy. It was almost impossible to get the clients to open up and share their agendas. Nonetheless, my contractor persisted in offering these brown bag luncheons in which she shared what she knew about critical developments in the field.

The brown bags attracted a regular following. Over the course of a year, a small community developed and they would often stay after the lunch concluded to talk a little about their work and the state of the industry. My customer stayed afterwards, too, and got to know these people well, cultivating the relationships and offering to help wherever she could.

The lunches were Value Pulses that created a platform of trust and dependability. When my client was ready to release a new service and promote it with force, she turned to this community to ask their ideas on how best to spread the word.

Based on the trust they had established, a new series of brown bags were designed that featured the new service front and center, describing the benefits this new service provided and explaining how it was relevant to the industry's needs. Each member of the community brought in a few colleagues and the briefing sessions experienced a surge of attendance that met the increase of information my client provided.

Because she was offering genuine value, people who attended the briefings were interested in connecting her to the places in their organization where she could make the most difference and she was able to drive significant uptake by following those leads. This is one example of a Value Surge at work.

Value Surges work for more than marketing. They can help clients apply new products and services to gain real results. This, too, drives uptake. They can also document successes, making it easier to identify exactly what results can be expected. This is another way to push greater acceptance.

Two Ways to Create Value Surges

1. Conduct a coordinated media blitz in which magazines, news channels, radio shows, Internet channels, newspapers, partner agencies and word-of-mouth instruments all fire simultaneously to create the effect of omnipresence. Arrange for the publication of concomitant

endorsements by multiple influencers, all pointing to your new or improved offering. This kind of blitz has the ability to reach your customers through multiple channels with reinforcing messages. As a result customers often move to the next threshold of engagement, driving uptake as they go. Be ready to assist in that regard. Go all out to help them get the results they are looking for.

2. Simultaneously release a group of products and services that reinforce each other; that is, multiply the benefits that clients can get when they are used together. Put them into clients' hands with assistance so the customer cannot help but experience the benefits. As this effort is taking place focus on getting results the client values, building the relationship, and driving uptake.

Timing is crucial for Value Surges. You want to be sure that market conditions are favorable. Keep in mind the experience from the customers' points-of-view. Take a look at the market as they experience it. Ask yourself, what conditions would amplify, accelerate, or expand the value that this surge will provide? Time your release to coincide with beneficial circumstances and you will increase the impact measurably.

Value Surges are all about speed and impact. When implemented with skill they create a central point of impact and a wave travels outward shifting everything in its path. Therefore you want to be well prepared so you can orchestrate implementation to be fast and influential. This means doing trial runs of the various systems required to be operational for success. For example, you must be ready to scale when there is the possibility of rapid uptake.

Scale Offerings with Value Webs

Value Webs are connected offerings that form synergies with each other. There are two important aspects of every Value Web: nodes and connections. The nodes are the discrete, identifiable products and services. The connections are the ways they interact with each other.

The example *du jour* is Apple's collection of products and services. Nodes include the products (iPod, iPhone, laptop, computer, iPad, and so on) and services (iTunes, iWork, and so on). The connections include local area networks, phone service networks (AT&T's network, Verizon's network), and iCloud.

When you buy your first iPhone, you have a smartphone: a sophisticated, highly customizable personal computer and communication device. If you then use it in combination with iTunes on your computer, suddenly your iPhone and computer can talk to each other and new functionality is available that goes beyond what either will do on its own. You can now pass music, videos, documents, and application data back and forth between computer and iPhone. Further, when you buy your spouse's iPhone, all three begin to interact. For example, if you write a grocery list on your iPhone in the reminders app, or on your computer, or on your spouse's iPhone, it automatically shows up on the other two. As you buy each successive Apple product or service, it enables the others in your possession to do more and more. The list of synergies feels endless.

This is how a Value Web works. Each individual offering becomes greater and more powerful with the addition of another. In the Value Web the whole is much greater than the sum of its parts.

Value Webs help you capture and hold customer share. As we can see from Apple's success, once the customer has invested in a host of products they are firmly established inside Apple's Value Web. They are much less likely to switch to another phone simply because it is cheaper or offers a better plan. When they switch they will lose the Value Web they have come to depend upon. They are also more likely to purchase new products Apple offers, and to look forward to the regular functional improvements Apple provides. This is how Value Webs drive uptake.

Four Ways to Create Value Webs

1. Provide a set of tools, applications, and services that are made to work together with some of the resulting features proprietary and only available from you.

2. Combine your service with exclusive deals provided by every vendor you associate with. Work out arrangements with your vendors to provide enhanced functionality to the customers who choose your service

3. Develop a branded club with training activities that increase your clients' capacity to handle business tied inextricably to other products and services you offer.

4. Construct a series of offerings at varying price points that work well together to create a sum total of experience and knowledge that advances your customers' success.

Value Webs are created by innovating on several fronts, providing an interconnected set of offerings that combine for greater result. As the nodes interact with each other through the connections, more and more value is realized and customers become ensconced. As a result they are more accepting, often eager and evangelical, of new ideas and offerings, taking them up with more speed and determination to put them to good use.

Value Pulses, Value Surges, and Value Webs are all specialized ways of delivering value to clients that drive uptake. Each positions you as the provider and builds relationships with your customers based on benefits they come to rely on and look forward to. In this way, you become a center of gravity, drawing clients to you who want what you have. This magnetism creates a virtuous cycle: clients come to you, they experience outstanding results, they associate those results with you, they come back and tell their friends, clients come to you, and so on. It is a major tool in driving uptake.

Powerful innovators are masters at driving uptake. They do not rely on chance or circumstance to succeed in the market. They are actively involved cultivating communities of buyers and building relationships that feed all their other activities: from discovering inflection points to generating value. This gives them an edge, puts them in contact with the heartbeat of their customers, and provides the relationships they require to drive uptake when it is time to deliver.

Success Rules

- Learn to bring your customers through the four thresholds of engagement: Attention, Investigation, Experimentation, and Identification.
- The best efforts to drive uptake depend on creating mutually satisfying goals built around a shared stake in success.
- When your innovations are fully aligned with what your customers value, they will do more than buy. They'll become evangelists.
- Innovations achieve uptake when their importance, significance, and value are shared.
- Build presence through Value Pulses; then accelerate growth through Value Surges.
- A Value Web is more than a collection of congruent items. Each offering synergizes the others, enabling new value that would not exist if each stood alone.

Appendix A

Sample Business Intelligence Contract

Note: This sample contract is not intended to represent a legal recommendation. Your legal counsel must approve your contracts.

Situational Summary

ABC INTERNATIONAL (ABC) wants to pursue active growth, increase revenues and profit, differentiate itself in the marketplace, and establish a brand that includes its well-deserved reputation for integrity and customer service.

Under the leadership of the current CEO, Julia Valdez, ABC has achieved significant growth systematically over the last nine years. To ensure continued growth it is necessary to secure business intelligence and act on it.

Objective

Gather the intelligence required to increase penetration in the marketplace.

Today there are 120 million customers that fit the ABC customer profile, yet ABC does business with only 25 million. This represents a significant opportunity for growth. Business intelligence will help define

1. Value-drivers that succeed in attracting those who are not yet customers.
2. Barriers to entry among the 95 million who are not yet customers.
3. Innovation initiatives that will support ABC to harvest a greater percentage of the market.

Measures of Success

1. ABC has in its possession intelligence that will increase customer base.
2. Due diligence has been conducted to include the perceptions and experience of staff, key customers, strategic partners, qualified prospects who have not become customers, market influencers, and thought leaders.
3. The results are analyzed and presented making clear options that provide ABC leadership with the knowledge they need to design and execute a customer development strategy.

Value to the Organization

Intelligence will inform the strategy to increase market penetration by

1. Expanding ABC's customer base
2. Providing greater influence and increased opportunities for innovation
3. Enabling innovations that increase profitable revenue generation

Methodology and Time Line

- March – April: Interview ABC staff and key customers, industry experts, thought leaders, qualified potential customers who have chosen not to invest, and influencers. Work together with CEO,

COO, and the senior team to identify and contact key sources of information.

- May–June: Prepare for and participate in the senior leadership retreat including sitting in on peer councils, running focus groups, meeting with key individuals for one-on-one interviews.
- July–September: Provide an interim report to the CEO, then determine: (a) what new developments must be taken into consideration, (b) how the results to date influence the information required to succeed, and (c) what changes if any are required to provide the best possible result.
- October: Work together under the guidance of CEO and COO to prepare a briefing for the November board meeting including identification of (a) market conditions, (b) challenges unique to the industry, (c) opportunity targets, and (d) recommendations for growth.
- November 18–20: Meet with the board to present and discuss recommendations.

Joint Accountabilities

This work will be a joint project carried out by ABC's CEO, Julia Valdez, and the XYZ Business Intelligence Agency under the CEO's supervision. Julia Valdez will provide

- Active participation and access to staff members and key partners as needed.
- Facilities, scheduling, and logistical support for any sessions to be conducted.
- Secretarial and administrative support for scribing and assembly of all documentation.

XYZ will provide

- Intellectual capital in the form of ideas, challenges, critique, and related discussions based on their experience with other organizations, leaders, and research.

- Leadership to drive the process including guidance on the development of a robust plan of action to achieve business growth.

XYZ will sign any nondisclosure agreements required to conduct business effectively. Both parties agree to immediately inform the other of any developments that might affect the success of this project. ABC agrees to support XYZ in executing the duties their role requires, which may include challenging conventional or accepted ways of carrying out work. In return, XYZ agrees to support all decisions made by ABC.

Terms and Conditions

Fee for this project: $99,999

ABC agrees to pay all travel, lodging, and meal expenses while traveling and to reimburse XYZ within 30 days of invoice date. XYZ assumes administrative fees associated with their work including any required duplication, fax, shipping, and postage.

This contract is non-cancellable for any reason, although it may be postponed and rescheduled at any time, with no penalty, subject only to mutually convenient time frames.

Acceptance

This proposal is accepted and forms an agreement between ABC INTERNATIONAL and XYZ Business Intelligence Agency.

Titles, names, signatures, and dates of responsible parties.

Appendix B

High-Level Outline of a Typical Business Plan

1. Executive Summary
   1.1. The Idea
   1.2. The Rationale
   1.3. The Business Case
   1.4. Success Factors
2. Statement of Purpose
3. Background
   3.1. Metrics
   3.2. Value
   3.3. Methodology
4. About Our Organization
   4.1. History
   4.2. Our Organization Today
   4.3. Mission
5. The Product and Its Market
   5.1. Strategic "Fit" with Our Mission
   5.2. Market Analysis: The Need in the Marketplace

Appendix C

Simplified Business Plan Financial Model

	A	B	C	D	E	F	G	H	I
1		new revenue (10% growth per year for five years)	2014	2015	2016	2017	2018		Five-year total
2									
3	Revenue								
4									
5	New products or services (@ $20,000)								
6	year one	500	$10,000,000						$61,051,000
7	year two	550		$11,000,000					
8	year three	605			$12,100,000				
9	year four	666				$13,310,000			
10	year five	732					$14,641,000		
11		3,053							
12									
13	Renewal income (@ $15,000)			$9,000,000	$13,545,000	$18,180,000	$22,950,450		$63,675,450
14									
15									
16	TOTAL REVENUE		$10,000,000	$20,000,000	$25,645,000	$31,490,000	$37,591,450		$124,726,450
17									
18									
19	Total purchases, assuming 60% new and 90% renewal		300	600	903	1212	1530		
20									
21									
22									
23		2012	2013	2014	2015	2016	2017		Five-year total
24									
25	Expenses								
26									
27	Test development and maintenance	$600,000		$5,000					$605,000
28									
29	Delivery	$150,000	$160,000	$170,000	$180,000	$190,000	$200,000		$1,050,000
30									
31	Marketing	$580,000	$330,000	$330,000	$330,000	$330,000	$330,000		$2,230,000
32									
33	Fulfillment	$1,200,000	$1,300,000	$1,450,000	$1,550,000	$1,700,000	$1,800,000		$9,000,000
34									
35	TOTAL EXPENSES	$2,530,000	$1,790,000	$1,965,000	$2,060,000	$2,220,000	$2,330,000		$12,885,000
36									
37	NET	($2,530,000)	$8,210,000	$18,045,000	$23,585,000	$29,270,000	$35,261,450		$111,841,450
38									
39	Note: Overhead has not been allocated. No inflation adjustment has been included.								

Notes

Introduction

1. Prusak, Larry. Action review of knowledge management: report and recommendations. World Bank, IBM Institute for Knowledge Management, Armonk, NY, 1999.

2. Internal World Bank document: TG 2.0 initiative: Communities of practice at the World Bank, 2008.

Chapter 1

1. Grant, Tim. Nonprofits, especially small ones, can benefit by nurturing diverse revenue sources. *Pittsburgh Post-Gazette*, June 29, 2012.

2. www.talknerdytome.net/2012/03/ipad-and-re-commerce-cnn.html

3. Rich, Laura. As I.T. goes, so goes Forrester? *New York Times*, February 18, 2005.

4. www.gazelle.com/media

5. Author's correspondence with HRCI.

6. www.avis.com.cy/We_try_harder.html

7. Martinez, Amy and Kristi Heim. Amazon a virtual no-show in hometown philanthropy. *Seattle Times*, March 31, 2012.

8. Dignan, Larry. Amazon posts its first net profit. CNET, January 22, 2002.

9. Martinez, Amy. Ibid.

10. How 'wichcraft multiplies its sandwich shops. Inc. www.inc.com/nicole-carter-and-tim-rice/how-wichcraft-multiplies-its-sandwich-shops.html

11. www.entrepreneur.com/article/199000

12. Ibid.

13. www.forbes.com/pictures/mjf45feid/6-tie-good-360-2/

Chapter 2

1. Davenport, Thomas H., Laurence Prusak, and H. James Wilson. What's the big idea? Creating and capitalizing on the best new management thinking. *Harvard Business Review Press*, 2003.

2. Strategic HR and innovation — creating the future: Insights by Holly C. Kortright. HR Certification Institute, 2011.

Chapter 3

1. Foreclosures (2012 robosigning and mortgage servicing settlement), New York Times online, April 2, 2012. topics.nytimes.com/top/reference/timestopics/subjects/f/foreclosures/index.html

2. Bartash, Jeffrey. Home rentals increase, and so do prices. Wall Street Journal, MarketWatch, April 30, 2012. articles.marketwatch.com/2012-04-30/economy/31491378_1_home-prices-home-ownership-rental-vacancies

3. Residential vacancies and homeownership in the first quarter 2012. U.S. Census Bureau News, April 30, 2012. www.census.gov/hhes/www/housing/hvs/qtr112/files/q112press.pdf

4. Bartash, Jeffrey. Ibid.

5. https://www.cia.gov/library/publications/the-world-factbook/geos/us.html

6. For example, Lee, Christopher. Transformational leadership in the new age of real estate. The Institute of Real Estate Management, 2012.

7. Tufte, Edward R. Visual explanations: Images and quantities, evidence and narrative. *Graphics Press* (February 1997).

Chapter 4

1. www.forbes.com/profile/philip-anschutz/

2. Shin, Annys. Anschutz has a low profile and large footprint. *Washington Post*, November 21, 2004, p. A1. sfppc.blogspot.com/2004/11/anschutz-has-low-profile-and-large.html

3. Last, Jonathan V. Pass it on: Meet Philip and Nancy Anschutz, winners of the 2009 William E. Simon Prize for Philanthropic Leadership. *Philanthropy Magazine*, Fall 2009. www.philanthropyroundtable.org/topic/excellence_in_philanthropy/pass_it_on

4. Ibid.

5. Martin, Roger L. The opposable mind: Winning through integrative thinking. *Harvard Business Review Press,* July 13, 2009. www.thinkers50.com/biographies/95

Chapter 5

1. www.kelloggcompany.com/company.aspx?id=39

2. www.kelloggs.com/en_US/our-history.html

3. How King Kellogg beat the blahs. *Fortune Magazine*, August 29, 1988.

4. Hagel III, J., J. S. Brown, D. Kulasooriya, and Dan Elbert. Measuring the forces of long-term change: The 2010 shift index. Deloitte Center for the Edge, 2010.

5. Hagel III. Ibid.

6. Correspondence between Panaggio and the author.

7. Conversation with the author.

8. The world in 2011, ICT facts and figures, ITU Telecom World, International Telecommunication Union.

9. Mobile factbook — April 2012, PortioResearch. www.portiorsearch.com

10. Sisario, Ben. A digital music option thrives, though quietly. *New York Times*, August 29, 2012. www.nytimes.com/2012/08/29/business/media/muve-music-for-mobile-users-thrives-in-shadow-of-competitors.html

11. Hindle, Tim. *Guide to management ideas and gurus.* Profile Books, Ltd. London, 2008.

12. Cornelius, Peter, Alexander Van de Putte, and Mattia Romani. Three decades of scenario planning in shell. *California Management Review*, Nov. 2005.

13. Conversation with John Kotter, March 2006. visionaryleadership.com /free-resources/leadership-interview-of-john-kotter-the-power-of-storytelling.php

Chapter 6

1. Weingarten, Gene. Pearls before breakfast. *Washington Post*, April 8, 2007. www.washingtonpost.com/wp-dyn/content/article/2007/04/04/ AR2007040401721.html

2. www.smithsonianmag.com/history-archaeology/copies.html

3. www.xerox.com/digital-printing/digital-printing-press/color-printing/xerox-igen-150/spec-enus.html

4. www.msnbc.msn.com/id/13245154/ns/us_news-life/t/tattoos-now-part-mainstream-culture/#.UEYchkKdYpk

5. www.lovemypetsgps.com/gps-dog-collar-page.html

6. www.trendhunter.com/trends/tub-collection

7. Wenger, E. Learning for a small planet: A research agenda. Sept. 2006. www.ewenger.com

8. www.jpl.nasa.gov/news/news.cfm?release=2011-390

9. abstracts.acs.org/chem/241nm/program/view.php?obj_id=61347&terms=

10. *Current Biology*, Volume 21, Issue 19, 1641–1646, 22 September 2011.

11. Zins, PhD, Gerald R. The history of the development of minoxidil. *Clinics in Dermatology*, Volume 6, Issue 4, October–December 1988, pp. 132–147.

12. articles.latimes.com/2012/feb/27/entertainment/la-et-oscars-main-20120227

13. www.eutimes.net/2012/07/eurozone-unemployment-rate-at-record-high-in-may/

14. www.britannica.com/blogs/2012/03/change/

15. Prensky, Marc, On the horizon. *NCB University Press*, Vol. 9 No. 5, October 2001. www.albertomattiacci.it/docs/did/Digital_Natives_Digital_ Immigrants.pdf

Chapter 7

1. www.cbsnews.com/2100-3445_162-2015684.html

2. Rogers, E. M. *Diffusion of innovations* (5th ed.). New York: Free Press, 2003.

3. Balestrero, Gregory. Global expansion and international partnerships. Project Management Institute, November 2, 2009.

Acknowledgments

My house has been an innovation lab this last year. In late 2011 my new daughter Ruchi joined our family, coming from a New Delhi orphanage at the age of six and speaking only marginal English. She gets the award for shifting perspective, making the transition from living on the street in India to a Pottery Barn bed in suburban Washington, DC, and all that entails.

My wife Laura has been my partner through it all. We are on a journey neither of us fully anticipated that is yielding the most precious of rewards: greater love for everyone involved. This last year has been a game changer and she has been my muse. Her soulful music has been especially helpful, carrying us both through the toughest times on the wings of her spirit (you can listen to her, too, at LauraBaronMusic.com).

Gabe, my son, accompanied me more than once on retreat where we listened to extremely loud music and pounded away on our keyboards in parallel satori or, at the opposite end of the spectrum, camped together in nature and talked about all that is most important in life (girls, religion, politics, and the meaning of life). True renewal either way.

I would also like to thank Larry Forster, who first brought me into Royal Dutch Shell. He taught me the power of friendship and its place in quality business thinking. On many long walks through the streets of Rijswijk and New Orleans we explored the challenges of systemwide change along with everything else life has to offer.

Larry and I share a love for the same Grimms's fairy tale, "Iron John." In it a traveler comes to a town and asks if there are any adventures to be had. The king directs him to a dark forest from which nobody returns. The voyager goes into this forest with his dog. While next to a pond a hairy hand comes out of the water, grabs the dog, and takes him down never to be seen again. "This must be the place," the adventurer says in response. And then he goes on to face what needs to be confronted. Many a time Larry and I would come to a roadblock or what seemed to be an impossible pass in our work together. We would look at each other and say, "This must be the place." Then we would go on to do the work necessary. We have always found our way to a happy ending (so far).

Sarah White (whitesarah.com) is the woman who midwifed this book. At one point during a key juncture in my writing she arranged for me to travel to a monastery close to her home. There she spent three days helping me intensively in relative seclusion. She did more than edit; she became my thinking partner. And it made all the difference in the world.

About the Author

Seth Kahan is an executive strategy consultant who works with CEOs to lead change and develop business innovations that improve market performance. He teaches over 25,000 professionals every year in conferences and professional seminars. Seth has provided leadership for large-scale innovation initiatives at Royal Dutch Shell, World Bank, and the Peace Corps, among many other organizations. In addition, he works with the CEOs of a large number of professional societies and trade associations to identify innovation that generates success for members while improving the bottom line, including the American Society of Association Executives, the Center for Association Leadership; American Geophysical Union; and the Human Resource Certification Institute.

He is the author of the *Washington Post* best-seller *Getting Change Right: How Leaders Transform Organizations from the Inside Out*. He writes regularly for Fast Company's website (SethFast.com), and his writing is syndicated to thousands of readers worldwide.

Seth lives in Bethesda, Maryland, with his wife, daughter, and son. Besides his family and work, he enjoys solo wilderness camping, traveling, poetry, and storytelling around the campfire.

For more information and to download Seth's articles on innovation and change leadership, visit VisionaryLeadership.com or facebook.com/GettingInnovationRight.

Index

Page references followed by f indicate an illustrated figure.